MY DARKEST HOUR

THE DAY I REALIZED I WAS ABUSIVE

A MEMOIR

Also by Harold L. Turley II

Born Dying
Confessions of a Lonely Soul
Love's Game

MY DARKEST HOUR

THE DAY I REALIZED I WAS ABUSIVE

A MEMOIR

HAROLD L. TURLEY II

SBI

STREBOR BOOKS

NEW YORK LONDON TORONTO SYDNEY

Strebor Books
P.O. Box 6505
Largo, MD 20792
http://www.streborbooks.com

ISBN 978-1-59309-287-0
LCCN 2009942983

First Strebor Books trade paperback edition April 2010

Cover design: www.mariondesigns.com
Cover photograph: © Keith Saunders/Marion Designs

10 9 8 7 6 5 4 3 2 1

Manufactured in the United States of America

For information regarding special discounts for bulk purchases, please contact Simon & Schuster Special Sales at 1-866-506-1949 or business@simonandschuster.com

The Simon & Schuster Speakers Bureau can bring authors to your live event. For more information or to book an event, contact the Simon & Schuster Speakers Bureau at 1-866-248-3049 or visit our website at www.simonspeakers.com.

*I dedicate this book to the woman who forced me to look
into the mirror and see the man I had become.
If I didn't, I would never have changed.*

*God blessed me with you so that I would be
able to help others overcome this disease.
There will never be a day that I will stop loving you.
You hold the key to my heart and dwell within my soul.*

You know who you are!

FOREWORD
A WORD FROM ZANE

When Harold first told me that he wanted to write a memoir about his experiences as an abuser, I was stunned. Not because I was not aware of domestic abuse. My book, *Breaking the Cycle*, deals with that very topic. However, I was surprised that such a humble, sweet-natured, excellent parent as Harold L. Turley II had abused someone. Then it made me think. The majority of the people who find themselves in these situations are not necessarily bad; they are dealing with issues that result in them lashing out verbally or physically and inflicting their own pain on someone else.

I am glad that Harold decided to write this book. There have been various books, both fiction and non-fiction, that were written about or by the abused. Rarely do we see one written by the person who victimized. It is a bold, heartfelt move and one that should not be taken lightly. Most abusers want to hide behind closed doors. They refuse to even admit that they have a problem. Even those serving prison time for domestic violence often deny their acts. Some may go through the motions of anger management and therapy while they serve their time, hoping to be paroled early. But even after all of that, the majority of them get released and abuse again.

Harold has faced his problems head-on and that is admirable. Hopefully this book will change someone. Hopefully this book will land in the hands of the men (and women) that need to read it the most: those who do the abusing. According to the American Bar Association, approximately 1.3 million women and 835,000 men are physically assaulted by an intimate partner annually in the United States. Those are not small figures. If you know someone who is being abused, please at least attempt to help them out of their situation. If you know someone that is abusing someone, make sure you give them this book. All of us must stop turning the other cheek to what we witness in this life. Sure, we can say that it is none of our business but that is a complete cop-out. I will be the first to admit that oftentimes abuse victims will reject help in the beginning. They are scared. They believe that they deserve it because the same thing happened in their household among their parents during their childhood. Some do not believe that they have any choice but to hang in there and hope they do not end up dead. But it only takes going too far one time.

According to the United States Department of Justice, between 1998 and 2002, of the almost 3.5 million violent crimes committed against family members, 49% of these were crimes against spouses and 84% of spouse abuse victims were females, and 86% of victims of dating partner abuse were female. Males were 83% of spouse murderers and 75% of dating partner murderers and 50% of offenders in state prison for spousal abuse had killed their victims. Wives were more likely than husbands to be killed by their spouses: wives were about half of all spouses in the population in 2002, but 81% of all persons killed by their spouse. Again, I cannot stress enough how vital it is to reach out to others and save them. It can begin with this book.

Harold L. Turley II has come forward and laid out a plan for an abuser to A) accept what they are doing and B) prevent themselves from doing it ever again. Not to say that this book alone can change a person but it can spark them into seeking the therapy they so desperately need. No one sets out to become an abuser and most of them are ashamed of their actions. But with therapy, prayer, and a solid support system, it is possible to change. Harold is living proof of that. Thanks for giving this book consideration and thanks for spreading the powerful message.

Blessings,

Zane

INTRODUCTION

BY HAROLD L. TURLEY II

I am writing this book in an effort to educate you on the signs, symptoms, and effects of abuse. I have lived a life full of abuse and because of it, those same abusive traits manifested within me without my own consent. I have been mentally and emotionally abused. I have been physically abused. I have been economically abused. I have even been spiritually abused. Not only have I endured these things, but I've also inflicted them upon others.

In our society, when dealing with any form of abuse, it is our initial reaction to help the person who is being abused. I do not disagree with this. However, what happens to the one who is committing the abuse? Who offers or provides help to that individual? Statistics say no one. So with that rationale, the person who is being abused gets help and can lead a healthy normal life. However, the person who commits the abuse doesn't; it only enables him or her to abuse someone else. The cycle doesn't stop until the abusive person gets help or is incarcerated.

Statistics also show that only ten percent of abuse cases are reported to the police, only ten percent. A record 20,992 cases of domestic violence were reported to police nationwide in 2007. If statistics are correct, out of these 20,992 reported cases of domestic violence, there were 188,928 cases that were not reported in 2007. This means only 20,992 men or women possibly will get help whether it is due to a judge forcing therapy or rehabilitation while incarcerated out of 209,920. This number is not acceptable.

This book was designed to offer help to 100 percent of men and women with abusive traits in an effort to try to stop this disease. My hope is that if you can see what I've gone through or what has happened within my life, it will make you take a look at your life and your actions. If you can see that you are traveling down the road to becoming abusive, hopefully together, we can pull the car over and stop you from going any further down that road of destruction.

This book was also designed for the men and women who are being abused. A lot of times, after we go through something so serious and severe, we isolate ourselves from society. I have found that a lot of times we tend to try to hold on to what has happened to us and not get the proper help we need in order to better deal with it. I am living proof of this. I also am living proof that if you continue with this way of thinking, the abuse will surely manifest within you, and you will, in turn, abuse someone else.

Some of you might ask, what are my credentials? What gives me the right to discuss such an important topic? Well, I'll be the first to tell you, if you are looking for a piece of paper or degree to validate my qualifications, you will be looking for a long time. I don't have one. I don't have a Ph.D. in psychology nor any other schooling on the topic. I don't work at a domestic abuse center or anything like that. What qualifies me to be able to speak on this are my life experiences. I've been on BOTH sides of the fence. I've felt the pain and effects of being someone who has been abused, as well as I've felt a different kind of pain after I, myself, abused someone else.

Let's be very clear, up front. I am in no way making excuses of any kind for why people abuse others. I do not in any way, shape, or form condone this behavior nor do I think it's acceptable. Every mistake that I have made in my life, I am in no way proud of it or boasting about it. However, let us also be clear that I do not regret any of the mistakes I've ever made, either. Regrets are mistakes that are not learned from. I have learned from my mistakes and that is my hope with this project. I hope that through my life, you can also learn from my mistakes so that you do not make the same ones. You may also see that you are the same person I was or that your spouse or partner is, and decide to get help.

Now after reading this, you might form your own opinions on my past mistakes and decide to never purchase another book I write. All of that is fine, but what I hope most is that you hear the message; you get the meaning behind the book. I pray that you allow yourself to open your mind and your heart to what is being said and then look at yourself in the mirror. Be honest with who matters most: YOU.

I will often reference the phrase "it's mirror time" within each review chapter of each stage. Use that time to take a very good, long, and hard look at yourself and ask yourself is this me or is this happening to me? I can't stress enough, please do not lie to yourself. This is for your benefit.

I'm not asking you to do anything that I haven't already done. This book originated as a therapeutic attempt for me. Writing is my escape from the world. I was the one who had to stand in front of my own mirror and take a very good, long, and hard look at myself and the man I saw wasn't me. I hated what I had become.

When I first started writing this, it started out as a way for me to express that hatred I had for myself. I wasn't the man my grandmother wanted me to be. I wasn't the man my mother wanted me to be. I was a vision of my past. I'd lost myself along the road of life and never even knew it. At that moment, I vowed to change. I didn't know how or where to turn or even what steps to take in order to regain myself again.

So I did the one thing that I did know: I got on my knees and prayed. I asked Christ to help me deal with the issues and problems that He had placed within my life. I knew that He was taking me through this for a reason. I needed Him to help guide me to do His will. Only with Him would I have been able to get through what I was experiencing and learn the lessons He set forth for me to learn. Once I did that, I felt calm enter my soul and take over my spirit. I could feel that I was on the road to recovery. I was on the right path. I wasn't on man's path but yet the path Christ had designed for my recovery.

I took out my laptop and began to express what I didn't like about me, where things had changed and where I felt I had started to go wrong. Page one turned into page seventy-five and within an instant a new journey had begun. As I read over what I'd put on paper, I realized that my story, my life experiences, might be able to help others. Especially other men, because we've seen the portrayal of abuse on TV over and over again, but the scene never changes. It's always the man who comes home and beats his wife or girlfriend for no apparent reason or the jealous husband who takes his rage out on his wife. We stigmatize that with physical abuse.

We, as men, think that because that isn't what we are doing that we aren't being abusive to whomever we are with. That is wrong. That isn't the only way to be abusive. So now we have a misconception of what abuse really is and we then continue to do what we feel as though we aren't doing. This leaves our partners with emotional scars. It's like a virus that spreads fast. Once we've implanted these emotional scars on our partners, statistics say when the relationship fails, they will then in turn do the same to their next partner.

Though there is no confirmed study that shows this behavior

is inherited, I believe it is to a degree. My belief is that it's a learned trait. It's not passed down through blood but rather exposure to it. And if you don't properly deal with the effects of being exposed to abuse at the onset, it will spread within your mind and become deemed as acceptable behavior. Not only by the person who is committing the abuse but in some cases the one who is being abused. Now they believe what they have endured is the other person's way of showing love, which then scars them for future relationships. They think the abuse inflicted is love so that is what they look for in their next partner.

This is what I call mental baggage or luggage. Relationships are just like trips. When you go on a trip, do you leave without taking anything with you? No, you pack a bag or some type of luggage. It's the same when you leave one relationship and go to the next. You take the baggage or luggage from that previous relationship into your new one. It could be something positive the prior person did that now has become the standard of your expectations in a relationship. Or it could be something negative that we characterize as love or him/her showing they care for us.

The negative baggage or luggage we take into our new relationships only hinders it and continues to take us further down the wrong path. Now your new partner is subjected to your mental baggage from the past relationship and is confronted with the same dilemma that you once were confronted with. If he or she doesn't correct it at the onset, or they come to believe what you have done is love, the abuse only continues to spread.

The stories told in this book are not fiction. They are real stories of different things and events that have happened to me. These stories are a part of my history and my make-up. Some are very explicit in detail and some have brief profanity. I try to keep the profanity to a minimum as much as possible. Please use caution when allowing teenagers to read this. Some need it; others might not be mentally ready. But no one knows your child better than yourself. Use your own judgment when making that call.

I am a devout Christian and I believe that through Christ all things are possible so I do reference the Bible and its teachings within this novel. Please keep in mind, these are my beliefs and do not have to be yours. This book was not intended to change your religious beliefs. If you are of the same faith as I am, please read the scriptures used within the book as reference material you can use within your everyday life. But, I want it to be known that by no means am I trying to force my religion upon any of you.

I hope everyone who reads this book finds it as an instrument that you can use within your everyday life when dealing with your significant other. I hope through my experiences, mistakes, and triumphs you can learn from them to help your everyday life. I'm a true believer that it takes a village to raise a child and we are all God's children. I am only doing my part within this village. I, by no means, am perfect but I strive for perfection. Every day I come up short but also each day I learn something new. I learn a new experience which in turn makes me a better man.

Before we can discuss a topic, we first must know what it truly means. There are three types of abuse we discuss within this book: emotional (mental abuse); economic; and physical (domestic abuse or domestic violence). The common word in each, however, is "abuse" or "abusive." Webster's Dictionary defines them as:

Abuse
- To put to a wrong or improper use
- Deceive
- To use so as to injure or damage
- To attack in words

Abusive

- Characterized by wrong or improper use or action: Corrupt
- Using harsh insulting language
- Physically injurious

1st Stage

EXPOSURE

**THE CONDITION OF BEING SUBJECT
TO SOME EFFECT OR INFLUENCE**

CHAPTER 1

PHYSICALLY BEATEN BUT MENTALLY ABUSED

The school year was finally winding down. The anticipation of summer was building up within me. The hot weather, fun at the pool, and no homework filled my soul. I couldn't wait. It wasn't like I didn't like school but I just needed a break from it. Today was a special day though. Today, we were having a half-day. I sat back and waited for 11 a.m. to roll around, for the bell to ring and for us to be dismissed to the buses. I was so ready to go.

This particular school week had been a very rough one for me. I'd recently gotten in trouble in class for going back and forth with a boy who I'd felt was disrespecting me. The usual teasing of a classmate was fine, but this was a little on the borderline. I still remember it as if it was yesterday.

"Harold, what do you plan on being when you grow up?" the teacher asked.

"Look at him, Ms. Adams, he isn't going to be much," Dwayne said.

"Shut up! I can be whatever I want," I quickly responded.

"Dwayne, I wasn't talking to you. I asked Harold. You will get your turn as well," Ms. Adams said.

"I'm sorry, Ms. Adams."

"Okay, fine. Now Harold, what do you plan on being when you grow up?"

"I don't know, Ms. Adams. I like a lot of things. I'm really into the show *Matlock* though. I'd love to be just like him and get innocent people out of going to jail."

"That's a pretty good profession. There are a lot of very good defense attorneys in the world. What do you plan on doing in order to make sure that you can be that when you get older?"

"What do you mean?" I asked.

"Well, next year you'll be going to middle school. That is where you need to start your preparation to become a defense attorney."

"How is that?"

"Well, in order to become any type of lawyer you have to go to college and then law school. High school is what sets all of that up for you, and middle school is what prepares you for high school. So when you leave here next year, you'll be starting your journey."

"Harold will never get into college, Ms. Adams. He is too dumb for that. Matlock! He would want to be some old white guy. Maybe you should think about being an actor because that is the closest you'll come to ever being any type of lawyer."

"Dwayne, that is enough!"

"Fuck you, Dwayne!" I shouted out as I stood up from my desk.

"Harold!"

Dwayne stood up from his desk as I started to approach him.

"I'm sick of his damn mouth. He always has something to say."

Ms. Adams quickly got in between both of us. She wanted to make sure the hazing didn't escalate into anything further.

"Naw, move, Ms. Adams. Harold has something he wants to get off his chest."

"Dwayne, go over there and sit down," Ms. Adams requested. Dwayne didn't move. He continued to stare me down. He knew he'd finally gotten to me and had me right where he wanted me.

"Dwayne, I said go over there and sit down."

Finally he did as requested and went to the desk at the back of the class. Ms. Adams grabbed me by the arm and escorted me out into the hallway. Once we were out the door, she said, "Harold, I'm very disappointed in you."

"I'm sorry, Ms. Adams. I'm just so sick of Dwayne always picking on me. I'm sorry but the longer I allow him to pick on me without standing up for myself, the more he is going to continue to do it."

"You are right. He will continue to do it but how is that hurting you. He can say whatever he wants to say. That in no way affects your life. The minute you start to listen to what he says, then that's when it starts to affect you. You know what you are capable of. You know what you can achieve and that is anything that you put your mind to. You are far more intelligent than this. Far more and I don't want to see this happen ever again. Do you hear me?"

Still angry, I was reluctant to reply.

"Harold, do you hear me?" Ms. Adams asked again.

"Yes, ma'am."

"I'm serious. I don't want to see you act like this again. You are far too bright for this. Now because of the language you used, I will have to write you up. I'll call your mom after school and let her know what happened."

"Do you have to, Ms. Adams?" I pleaded.

"Harold, do you cuss around the dinner table at home?"

"Humph... what dinner table? We aren't the Cosbys. I usually eat my dinner in the living room or in my bedroom."

Ms. Adams couldn't help but laugh. "Boy, I swear! What am I going to do with you? You know what I mean. Plus, if I let you use that language in my class and there are no repercussions, then everyone is going to think they can as well. I have to set the example and the standard of what is acceptable and what is not."

"Okay, okay, but do you have to call my mom? She is going through enough as it is already, Ms. Adams," I replied.

"Aren't we all, and yes, I do need to call her. Plus, I need her to monitor your behavior at home. We need you to become that defense attorney when you get older, remember?"

"Yes, I remember."

"Now, are you okay to go back to class or would you rather go sit in Ms. Hughes' class until dismissal so that you can calm down?"

"I'm fine," I replied.

"Well, I think you'll be best in Ms. Hughes' class."

"Why would you ask me if you already had your mind made up on what I was going to do?"

"Because I can…now go ahead and sit down in Ms. Hughes' class. I will have Jasmine come over and bring you your book bag and stuff. Think about what I said, too, Harold. The only thing that can ever hold you back in life is you and your temper. You can't allow anyone to have that type of power over you."

I SAT IN MS. HUGHES' CLASS THINKING ABOUT ALL THAT MS. ADAMS HAD SAID. I knew she was right and knew I needed to work on my temper. It didn't matter what Dwayne thought of me or what he had to say. He was nothing but what my grandmother called a road bump in life. They are placed on the road to slow you down, so you do as they are meant for. You slow down, but you continue to keep pressing forward to your destination. When you can understand the true meaning of a road bump, then you can appreciate its use and not look at it as something negative.

The dismissal bell rang and I headed to my bus. The minute I saw Dwayne sitting in the front of the bus, I should have not gotten on. He didn't ride my bus. He lived in another part of the neighborhood that had its own bus, but instead of listening to my inner voice of reasoning, I decided to get on the bus. I would just ignore him and whatever he had to say.

Shockingly, during the ride home from school, Dwayne didn't have anything to say. I sat in the back of the bus talking to my best friend, John, about our weekend plans. He was having a birthday party and I was hoping Ms. Adams' call to my mom wouldn't keep me from being able to attend. I always had fun at John's house. It was my escape from the constant arguing I heard at home between my mom and her boyfriend.

We finally reached the bus stop and everyone started to get off the bus. The closer I got to the front, the more I started to realize everyone crowding around like a fight was about to happen. I knew I should have listened to my inner voice. They say a hard head makes for a soft ass, and I was the perfect example.

I'd been in plenty of fights so it wasn't as if I was scared. You win some and you lose some, but as long as I stood up, then I'd be respected. If I won, of course I'd get more respect, but just by fighting, I'd get the respect that he knew I wasn't going to run. If it was a fight he wanted, I was going to happily oblige.

I stepped off the bus and there was Dwayne patiently waiting for me.

"You had all that mouth in class; now you don't have Ms. Adams to save you," he said.

"Look, I don't have time for this. You aren't even worth it. What you think or have to say doesn't even matter. You are irrelevant."

"Fuck you, you lil' bastard! You don't even live around here.

You walk your ass from here to the fucking projects like we are stupid. You and your retarded-ass best friend, and you have the nerve to talk."

I could feel the anger boiling inside of me. The more Dwayne started to insult me, the more it would rise until walking away was no longer an option.

"Come on, let's just go," John said.

"Yeah, you and your retarded-ass friend need to head back home to the roaches."

Before Dwayne could say another word, I'd swung. I'd punched him with a straight right hand to his mouth. He staggered back and the blood started to trickle down from his mouth. I was full of rage, so full of rage, I never saw the blindsided punches to follow from his friends helping him. The next thing I remember was being in the fetal position trying my best to cover my face. My body was badly battered from the kicks. My right eye was cut and closed shut. They'd really worked over me and my best friend also, as he tried to help defend me.

Dwayne was correct. We didn't live in the same neighborhood as the other kids. John lived in the next apartment complex over. I lived a little further away. Though we all were on the poverty line in one way or another, I was a little more fortunate than them. My mother owned her own house. She wasn't renting an apartment. I didn't live in Dwayne's apartment complex or John's, but I chose to keep that to myself and allowed the kids to assume what they wanted. All they knew was that I didn't live in their neighborhood, and in my mind, whose neighborhood I lived in was none of their business.

Once the dust settled and the beating was over, John helped me to my feet so we could head home. I could hardly walk, I was in so much pain. My eye was throbbing and I could barely see. I caught the brunt of the beating. John was bruised as well but not as much as I was. It was as if a point was trying to be made to me.

Once we reached John's house, I couldn't walk anymore. I needed to rest up. I was in too much pain. I thought maybe I needed to call my mom and let her know what had happened and say that I'd be at John's house for a little bit. But then I thought against it. There was no telling if Ms. Adams had already talked to her, so she probably wouldn't believe me until she got home and saw the evidence of the attack herself. Plus, it was still relatively early in the day since we had an early dismissal. It wasn't as if she would be home anytime soon either. I could just stay until we regularly got off the bus and then head home. I'd still beat her there so it wouldn't a problem.

I'd been through enough. I needed something to smile about. After an ass whipping like that, who wouldn't need to? John and I played video games for the rest of the afternoon. It was just what I needed. I knew my mother would flip the minute she saw what had happened to me. She was an old-school mom. You didn't put your hands on her child without hearing about it. I knew she'd want to go up to the school and talk to Dwayne, his parents and anyone else who would listen. And if any of them had a problem with it, then she would become their new problem.

I left John's house and headed home. Once I finally reached there, to my surprise, my mom's boyfriend was there. Normally, he came home after my mother did. I definitely wasn't expecting him to be there, but he hardly paid me any attention so I wasn't really worried. He more than likely was in the bedroom asleep or drinking. He probably wouldn't even know I was in the house until hours later. I could go to my room and take a nap until my mother stormed in, wanting to talk about my behavior in class earlier.

I opened the door and Stanley was sitting on the couch. Once I closed the door, he got up and headed toward me.

"Where have you been? School let out hours ago."

"I was at my friend John's house. I'd gotten into a fight earlier today and needed to clean up and rest a bit."

"Do you think I care? Your mom told you that you are supposed to have your ass home right after school, RIGHT AFTER. Not when the fuck you want to come in here. You don't pay any gotdamn bills!"

"I'm sorry. I didn't think it would be a big deal. I'll explain everything to Mommy when she gets home," I responded.

Faster than a blink of an eye, Stanley punched me in my mouth. The power of the blow knocked me off my feet. Tears begun to well up in my eyes.

"Just like a little bitch! Go ahead and cry. That's probably how you got your ass whipped earlier. Bitches don't know how to fight. That's okay; I'll make a man out of you, one way or another. I don't care if I have to beat it out of you."

"Stanley, please stop! Just leave me alone," I said as I tried to get up and make my way to my room without further confrontation.

He grabbed me by my shirt collar, choking me, and then threw me into the front door. The more I screamed, the more he struck me. Finally, my cries for help started to annoy him. He went into the back room and came back into the living room with a ping-pong paddle in his hand. He flipped me upside down and pulled my pants down. He then held me by my ankles and beat me with the ping-pong paddle as if it were a belt. If I tried to put my hands in the way of my butt, the paddle would crack my knuckles. I had to pick which pain I wanted to endure: either the pain of the paddle hitting my butt, or the pain of the paddle cracking across my knuckles.

This went on for what seemed like hours instead of fifteen minutes. By the time he was done, I'd forgotten all about my eye. It was no longer in pain. My ribs, badly bruised from being jumped, no longer hurt either. My new wounds overtook all of that. Tired from his workout, Stanley finally released my ankles, dropping me to the floor. Every word he spat out during the beating fell on deaf ears. I didn't hear a word. I didn't see a blow; all I remember was crying out for it to stop. Wondering what I'd done to ever deserve any of it.

Stanley then looked at me and said, "Now get your ass up and get your chores done. Wash those dishes and get that trash out before your mom gets home. I don't feel like hearing her bitch tonight."

He was talking to me as if what he had done was acceptable. I couldn't believe it. He sat there and beat me like he was facing a man on the street and then turned around and that was the very next thing he said. Scared, I got up and went into the kitchen. I quickly washed every dish and took out the trash. I didn't want to upset him any further.

My mother always knew I couldn't stand Stanley because of how he talked to her but never did I have enough to make her leave him. Finally, I had all that I needed. The minute I finished my chores, I went straight to my bedroom. I didn't want any more confrontations with Stanley. Just the smallest thing could set him off and the next beating might kill me.

All I could do was sleep. I lay down and fell straight asleep. I was emotionally drained. All the crying had taken its toll on me. I didn't wake up until my mother came into my room when she finally came home from work.

"Harell," my mother called. That was her name for me. I was named after my father and never answered to "Junior" so she came up with "Harell."

"Harell! I know you hear me calling you," she repeated.

This time I woke up from my deep sleep. I turned over and faced her. The minute I saw her face, I broke out into tears again. My mother couldn't help but notice my battered face.

"What happened to you?" she asked.

I then began to confess everything. I told her what had happened earlier in class. I told her about getting jumped after I got off the bus and then going to John's house. Then I told her about the beating I received when I got home. Piece by piece, I told her everything. Each time I'd connect a new puzzle piece to what had transpired earlier in the day, the more appalled she became. It wasn't until I told her what Stanley had done that she broke down. She just grabbed ahold of me and started to comfort me.

All that I'd done wrong earlier in school had been forgotten. My mother's motherly instincts kicked into overdrive and all she could do was comfort her firstborn.

"Everything is going to be okay. I will take care of everything, I promise!"

"Ma, I just want to move. I want to go live with Grandma. I just want to move. I don't want to be here anymore," I pleaded.

"I will take care of everything. I promise, Harell. Everything will be okay," my mother said.

She then turned and left out of my room, fuming. She headed into her bedroom to confront Stanley about his behavior. I couldn't clearly hear the argument. I eased out of my door into the hallway, hoping to be able to hear the argument better. I just knew my mother would either tell Stanley to leave or that we were leaving. I didn't hear either. All I heard was Stanley's excuses for his actions. First he lied about what he did. He denied punching me or fighting me. He denied just about everything. He denied picking me up by my ankles and beating me with a ping-pong paddle. Instead he told her that I had gotten smart with him and said that I didn't have to answer to him. He then asked me to do my chores and I told him that I didn't have to do anything, so he got a belt and spanked me.

I knew my mother wouldn't fall for that though. I had a very good imagination but there was no way I could make any of that up. Not to that degree; my mind wasn't that advanced at such a young age. She had to know that I was telling the truth and she was being conned by an abusive man. But to my surprise, the next thing I heard was, "You know I love you and Harell, and I would never do anything to jeopardize any of that." And just as quickly as she had become outraged about what I had told her, she did a 180-degree turnaround and fell into Stanley's trap.

CHAPTER 2

WHEN ENOUGH TRULY BECOMES ENOUGH

O ver the years, things hadn't gotten any better between my mom and Stanley; instead they'd only gotten worse. I no longer was being abused by Stanley. After my first encounter with him, I guess he thought that was enough. He knew to a degree that I feared him. He knew there was no need to do any more. His primary target now was my mother. She had a very hard spirit to break and he spent every waking day trying to. Argument after argument, fight after fight, continued throughout my childhood. The fact that she decided to marry him only made the situation worse than what it originally was.

The only difference was now I was a sixteen-year-old man. I know, those terms don't go hand in hand. Sixteen and man, no sixteen-year-old should ever be considered a man. He is still a child in the world's eyes. But based upon the things that I had already endured from age eleven, sixteen qualified me as a man. Call it life's experience that gave me the qualification.

I had long given up on trying to break up my mother and Stanley. I knew there was nothing I could do. She was deep in confusion which she mixed up with love. I knew she wouldn't leave until she was ready to leave and at that point and time, I couldn't see that day ever coming. I prayed it wasn't death that did them part. Ironically, I didn't even wish death upon Stanley. Call it my grandmother's heart to forgive a part of me. I don't know. But what I did know was that I only had two more years left to endure the hell of living within that house. I didn't want to leave my mother, but I knew if I stayed, I would lose what was most important to myself: ME.

I tried to stay as busy as possible. I made it a point to never be at home. I ran the streets so much you could easily come to the assumption that I lived on them. It didn't matter how much my mother disapproved. Any excuse not to be in the house, was my excuse and if I didn't have one I would make one up. I would go from house to house; it didn't matter. People would often question why I didn't want to go home or ask what was wrong, but I would never tell them. I knew enough to know that you don't put people in your business. That only makes matters worse. Plus, this wasn't just my business to tell. Actually, it was my mom's. It had stopped being mine a long time ago.

I pulled up in front of the house a little after 1 a.m. Shockingly, Mom's car wasn't out front. That was odd for a Wednesday night. Especially since tomorrow wasn't any type of holiday. Stanley's, of course, was there. I thought maybe they had gone out together or something. But, then I thought if they had, who was watching my younger brother and sister. My brother was only nine and my sister was seven. It wasn't like they could watch themselves.

Regardless what the situation was at hand, I was tired. I still had to get up early in the morning to head to school and start the day of events all over again. I went inside the house. While I was in the kitchen getting a glass of water, Stanley walked in.

"Oh, I thought you were your mother."

I didn't reply.

"Have you talked to her?"

I shook my head no and finished drinking my water.

"Where has your ass been?" he questioned.

"Out!" I quickly snapped back.

Though I stood nearly six-feet-two at age sixteen, I had the body of a teenage boy. I was barely one hundred and twenty pounds. I was very slender but my heart was much bigger. A part of me was looking for the perfect confrontation with Stanley. I hadn't forgotten being picked up by my ankles and beaten. Never would I forget that.

Stanley grabbed my arm. He reeked of vodka.

"Lil' nigga, who the hell do you think you are talking to?"

I quickly pulled my arm from his grasp and stood there. I stared at him, waiting for him to make the next move. He started to laugh.

"Let me find out you finally have some balls. It's about time your bitch ass turned into a man."

I ignored his comment and walked out of the kitchen. I was ready for anything he was going to try, but I wasn't going to initiate it. I wasn't going to give him the satisfaction of saying he was defending himself. He would never get that pleasure because the next time he put his hands on me, the cops were definitely coming. Self-defense wasn't going to be an option he would be afforded to use, IF he even needed one.

I went into my bedroom and turned on the TV. Nothing was really on, but I was still pumped up full of adrenaline so there was no way I could've lay down and gone to sleep. The way I was feeling, I could've punched a hole through the wall. I took my clothes off and started to get ready to unwind.

The second I started to close my eyes was when I heard the front door close. I glanced up at the clock. An hour had passed that quickly. It was almost 2:30 a.m. I didn't think anything of it until I heard Stanley come out of the bedroom.

"Where the hell have you been at?" Stanley questioned.

"The last time I checked, I was grown. I don't have to check in with you. I went out with Daphne and Michelle."

"The fuck you mean, you went out? Don't you know the kids were in here? I have to get up early in the morning."

"Then why is your ass up? And what do the kids have to do with anything? The last time I checked, you were their daddy, too. You should be able to handle cooking dinner every once in a while. Shit, it's not like you do it every night or something."

"Linda, I don't want to hear that shit. You have been out more and more the last couple of months. Is it some other guy?"

"What?"

"You heard me; I'm not getting any of your time, so someone is. Who is he?" Stanley asked again.

"Why?, What you concerned for? This damn sure isn't a marriage we are in. Why do you care if some other man treats me the way you should be? I have to get it from somewhere. I deserve to be loved and if you damn sure enough aren't going to do it, why not find someone else who will?"

"Oh really? Are you sleeping with him, too?"

"Don't ask a question that you really don't want to know the answer to, Stanley."

"I'm not going to ask you again. Are you fucking him?" Stanley reiterated.

"What I do is no longer any of your business. It's a little too late for you to try to be a husband now. Where was my husband when I needed him for me? Where was he when the bills needed to be paid? All you do is spend your money on booze. That is your concern—vodka. You aren't concerned about a wife, so as far as I'm concerned, you don't have one. Now would you please move? I'm tired. I have had a very long night and I still have to be to work in the morning. Someone has to pay the bills around here, so the house doesn't go into foreclosure. It damn sure enough isn't going to be you."

The next thing I heard was a loud thump and my mother started to cry. Then I heard something being banged into the wall. I couldn't stay in my room any longer. I jumped out of my bed and ran out to see what was going on. I saw Stanley choking my mother up against the wall.

"Who the hell do you think you are talking to? You aren't going to disrespect me in my own house!" Stanley shouted.

"Get your hands off my mother!" I yelled.

My mother looked at me with fear in her eyes. "Baby, it's okay. Go ahead back to bed. It's okay," she said as Stanley's hands were still around her throat.

I didn't want to hear any more from either of them. It might have been acceptable to her, but it damn sure enough wasn't for me; regardless of what she said. My natural reflex was to swing. I hit Stanley with a punch to the side of his head with all my might. Trying to defend himself from my blows, he let go of my mother and tried to cover himself up so I couldn't get a clean shot on him. My mother tried to stop me and jumped in between Stanley and me.

"Move, Ma," I said as I pushed her out of the way.

She fell to the floor and I diverted my attention back to Stanley. By now, he was charging me and picked me up off of the floor and slammed me to the ground. He outweighed me by over one hundred pounds. My mother came to my aid, stopping Stanley from kicking me while I was on the floor. He then punched her in the face, sending her back into the wall.

"Have you lost your mind?"

He grabbed her and started choking her again. His back, however, this time was turned toward me as I was no longer a part of his attention. I grabbed the closest thing I could find, which was a stereo speaker, and picked it up and hit Stanley on the back of his head with it. The pain from the blow was evident as Stanley cried out in agony. He dropped down to one knee but that didn't stop my attack. I hit him again and again with the speaker. Then when he was totally down, I started to kick him over and over again. I didn't hear my mother's pleas for me to stop. I didn't hear anything. All I saw was my rage at full tilt as I let Stanley know he was no longer in charge.

Finally, my mother was able to get me to stop. She pulled me back and into my room.

"He shouldn't have put his damn hands on you. No one puts their hands on you. I don't give a damn about that man."

"Baby, he is still your stepfather. This is not your fight. He didn't mean to hit me. I pushed him too far. I shouldn't have said all that I did. I made him hit me."

"What! Ma, have you lost your mind? You can't make anybody do anything. He didn't make me hit him. I hit his ass because I wanted to. Now, yes, his actions led to mine but I had the choice. I knew exactly what I was doing. I allowed my anger to get the best of me, the same as he did with you."

My mother started to cry. Stanley burst into my room. I quickly grabbed for the pistol that I had hidden under my pillow on my bed and pulled it on him.

"Harrell!" my mother cried.

"What are you going to do with that?" Stanley asked.

"You come a step closer and you surely will find out. You put your hands on my mother EVER again and you will find out. You touch one hair on my brother and sister and you will find out. Do you hear me? Do I make myself clear?"

"Do you think I'm scared? You don't have the balls to pull the trigger."

I laughed. "Just like I didn't have the balls to beat the shit out of you a minute ago, too, huh? If you want to try me, Stanley, go right ahead. I've said all I have to say."

I looked at Stanley, waiting for him to make his next move. He turned to my mother and said, "I'm out of here. Forget you and your crazy-ass son!"

He turned to head out of the door.

"Stanley, wait!" my mother cried.

"Ma!" I said, grabbing her to stop her from running after him. "Let his ass go. We don't need him, Ma."

"That is my husband, baby. He is my husband," she said. "Stanley, wait. Can we just talk about things? Please, come on into the bedroom and let's just talk."

"For what? You've said all that you had to say. Go and talk to the guy you've been sneaking around with behind my back."

"Please, I'm sorry. There is no other man. I have been spending a lot of time out with the girls. I swear. I just wanted you to be jealous and think it was another man, hoping things would change at home. Please, can we just talk?" she pleaded.

"Fine," Stanley said and looked at me with a grin.

I couldn't believe what I'd just seen. I knew that might not have been hers, but it damn sure was my last straw. I went into my room and grabbed my pants from off my desk chair where I'd laid them when I first got in. I put my pants on, tucked my pistol in my waistband and grabbed my car keys.

"Where do you think you are going?" my mother asked sternly.

"Ma, you made your choice. I just pray to God, He watches over the kids because they don't deserve to grow up like this. I refuse to any longer, though. I'm out."

"Harold Leonard Turley II, I am still your mother and you will respect me in my house."

I turned and looked at her.

"How can you demand respect from me within your house when you don't even respect yourself? But that is part of your problem. Actually, both of yours; neither of you know what respect really is."

I turned back and headed for the door.

"If you walk out of that door, don't come back. Do you hear me? If you leave out of this house, you better not return!" she demanded.

I couldn't help but laugh. "This is far from a house, but don't worry. I won't!"

I walked out of the front door. I headed to the only place I knew where to get peace—my best friend John's house.

CHAPTER 3

THE POWER OF WORDS

I didn't feel like going to school one day. I had a lot on my mind. Things between my mother and me were far from right. It had been a little over a year since the last incident I'd had with Stanley. After that, I stayed at John's and my grandmother's for a couple of days before my grandmother talked me into going home. I wanted to tell her all that was going on, but I didn't know how. Instead, I kept it all boiled up inside of me and made it seem as if it was a normal dispute between my mother and me.

In that instance, how could she not see that her daughter wasn't correct? My grandmother would always say, "Your mother is always right, even when she is wrong." I couldn't even help but laugh. I never understood what she meant by that, but I figured one day she'd explain it to me because there is no way one person can always be right. Everyone is wrong some of the time and most people are most of the time.

Thankfully, I had met Lena. She was exactly what I needed to get my mind away from the troubles I was going through at home. A person could only play basketball but so much and I wasn't going to spend every waking minute at John's house. I needed another outlet and my woman was just that. She kept me sound and definitely sane. She knew how to keep me laughing. She was the perfect remedy in my eyes. She was my angel.

I decided to skip school that day and stay at John's house. His mother finally moved into a house that was only a few blocks away from the high school. That made skipping school relatively easy. All I would do was drive to school and park in the school lot, then walk to John's house. Just in case his parents came home early, I didn't want my car to be parked in front of the house giving everything away. Plus, it wasn't as if our school security would do anything if they saw me leaving. They didn't really care who came and who left. They spent the bulk of their time trying to get the high school girls to leave school early with them.

I'd reached John's house and he already had the front door opened and waiting on me.

"What's going on?" John asked me as I walked into the house.

"Nothing much, I see you are dressed."

"Yeah, I'm not staying here with you. I have a test today in English class so I can't miss it. I might leave during second period. I'm not sure yet."

"That's what's up. I'll probably just lie around and watch some movies then."

"Where is Lena? She's not going to chill here with you?"

"I'm not sure. She might walk over after school, but I doubt she leaves school to come over."

"Why not? I don't know what is wrong with you. As much time as you spend with her, if I were you, I would have hit that by now. I swear, I don't know what you are waiting for."

I started to laugh. "Is that all you think about?"

"What else is there to think about?"

"Obviously, nothing else for you but I'm different. I'm not really tripping off that right now. When the time is right, it will be right. Right now, I just enjoy spending time with her. It beats being at home and hearing my mom and her husband argue all the time."

"Don't you mean your stepdad?" John asked.

I gave him a look, as if his statement wasn't funny.

"Don't play with me. That man is nothing to me but my mother's husband and my brother's and sister's father. Outside of that, he is irrelevant. Never forget that!"

"Yeah, yeah! Let me ask you something. If you hate him so much, how come you don't just tell your dad how he treats you and your mom? I'm sure he'd say something to him for you."

"Naw, I doubt that. I'm far from my dad's concern. All he is worried about is making sure he makes the child support payments on time to my mom. Outside of that, it doesn't even matter. I hardly even see or talk to him anymore. I used to go over and see him in the summer but that stopped the older I got."

"Well, you need to tell someone! You can't just keep it inside of you. It's not healthy. I still say you call the cops or call your dad. Shoot, give him the opportunity to do nothing first. Then if he doesn't, then go to someone else, but you don't need to be going at this alone by yourself."

"I'm not alone. I have you. I tell you everything so I'm getting it off my chest."

"But what am I going to do? I can't help you and that is what you need," John shot back.

"Look, John, I'm going through enough right now. I really don't feel like hearing this. Please, just leave it alone. It is what it is."

"No, it's not; it is what you make it to be, but fine. I will leave it alone for now. Plus, I have to get out of here and get to class, but we'll finish this later on."

"No, we are not. I don't want to talk about this anymore. The school year is almost over anyway and I'll be graduating in a couple of months. The minute I graduate, either I'll get a job and get my own apartment or I'll join the military. Either way, I will be out of that house and it will no longer be a problem, so you don't have to worry."

"What happened to you wanting to go to college and being a defense attorney?"

"What are you talking about?"

"What? That was your dream and you forgot."

"I don't know what you are talking about."

"Wow, yeah, you really need help then. I still remember the day we got jumped around Southview by Dwayne and his boys. It was all over you telling Ms. Adams you wanted to be like Matlock when you grew up. That was what? Sixth grade. Yeah, it sure was."

"Damn, you are right. I remember that. That was the day I came home and got the worst ass whipping of my life. Yeah, a lot changed that day, John, a lot!"

John could see the pain in my eyes. He didn't want to push me too far. He knew he was the only one who had a chance at getting me to get help, so he didn't want to lose that capability by pushing me away.

"Look, I'm about to be late. Let me get out of here. If you decide to leave, just lock the bottom lock. I lost my top lock key."

"I'm not going anywhere. I'll be here when you get back, but if by chance I do roll out, I got you."

"Thanks!" John said, then headed toward the front door. He turned back to me. "I thought you said Lena wasn't coming over."

"She isn't," I replied.

"Then who is that right there walking this way?"

I got up off the couch and headed toward the front door. He was right. Lena was walking toward John's house. I'd mentioned to her the previous night that I wasn't going to go to school the next day, but she kept saying she'd see me after school. I guess she changed her mind also.

"Damn, I guess you are right. I didn't plan on seeing her until later on."

"Well, looks like you will be able to see ALL of her today," John said and then started laughing.

"I already told you how I felt about that," I replied.

"Yeah, whatever. I'm out!"

John headed out the front door just as Lena approached the steps.

"Good morning to you, Ms. Lena. How are you this lovely day?"

"You are awfully chipper this morning. I'm fine. You still are going to school?"

"Yeah, I have a test this a.m., but I'll probably be back later on after that. Will you still be here?"

"Get your mind out of the gutter, boy, and go take your test," she snapped back at him.

Lena walked into the house.

"Hey, baby," she said.

I gave her a hug. "What are you doing here? I thought last night you said you'd see me after school."

"Is there a problem with me coming over or did you have plans or something? I know how John thinks. What, y'all had some girls coming over later or something?"

"Lena, please do not start with me. No, I just wasn't expecting you until later, is all. It's fine. I'm actually glad you came over. Why do you always have to take things to another level?"

"Because, I don't trust how your little mind works. That is okay though. I wish another chick would come over here while I'm here. I definitely have something for her."

"Lena, stop! There is no one else. No one is coming over here. You are all that I need," I said, reassuring my love for her.

"I better be!"

As TIME WENT BY, WE SAT AROUND TALKING AND WATCHING MOVIES. She was in love with *The Lion King*. Don't ask me why. That was more like something my little sister would want to see instead of her but it was cool. I hadn't been getting much sleep anyway and that was the perfect movie to knock me right out. We lay on the couch and cuddled while she watched the movie and I slept, holding her.

It wasn't until she turned over and started to kiss me on my neck did I awake. The feel of her lips on me started to turn me on. I wasn't a virgin so it wasn't as if I was scared to have sex, but more so I just didn't want to rush things with Lena. Our relationship was special. I didn't want to ruin it with sex. Once we took things to the next level, it could easily turn the relationship focus to sex only.

"What are you doing?" I asked.

She continued to kiss me. "What do you think I'm doing?"

"Baby, I know what it is you are doing, but we've already talked about this. You know I want us to take things slow. I don't want to rush things."

Lena jumped up off of the couch.

"I don't get you. Here it is, most of the boys in school would be begging to get some and I'm offering it to you, but you don't want it. And then you wonder why I think you are cheating. If you don't want to do me, it must be because you are doing someone else."

"Lena, would you please stop? There is no other chick. We can easily do it now, and then what? We do it every time we see each other? I'm sorry but that doesn't seem like fun to me. I enjoy spending time with you. I enjoy us laughing, us talking. What is wrong with that?"

"What about Asia? You had no problems doing it to her. You weren't interested in just talking to her."

I looked at Lena, puzzled.

"Where did that come from? Who cares about Asia? I damn sure don't; that is why it was nothing. It meant nothing. Don't you understand? You mean something to me. Why would you want to be treated like a woman who means nothing? What thrill do you get out of that?"

"What is it? Is she prettier than me? Maybe you just aren't attracted to me. Is that it, Harell? You just aren't attracted to me?"

"Baby, would you please stop. I think you are beautiful. I think you are amazing. I love everything about you. Some nights I just sit back and thank God for bringing you into my life. Especially at a time like right now with all that I'm going through at home. You have to believe me. There is no chick out here who can replace you with me. I don't want any of them other chicks in school. I don't want Asia or anyone else. Yes, she and I had sex way before you, but all I was looking for with her was pleasure, not a lifetime friendship. I wasn't looking to build anything with her."

"How are we building anything if you don't want to even have sex with me? If you really want to show me how much you love me, you know how."

Lena started to take her shirt off.

"Lena, me having sex with you doesn't show you how much I love you. It doesn't show you anything at all. I really wish you could see that," I said and then headed toward the front door.

Lena jumped in front of me.

"What? You are going to just leave? Well, then go ahead and leave, you weak bastard. That is okay; I don't need you to do anything with me. There are plenty of men I can get to screw me. I just wanted to be with you, but please believe I won't make that mistake anymore. I was a fool for even wasting my time with a nigga like you. You aren't even worth it."

"How are you going to just sit there and talk to me like I'm nothing?" I asked.

"Because that is exactly what you are. You are *nothing* to me!"

I couldn't believe my ears. I needed to get out of there and fast.

"Move, please, so I can go," I said.

"I'm not moving anywhere and you aren't going anywhere either. I'm not done talking to you."

"I don't want to hear anything else you have to say. I've heard all that I need to hear."

"You don't run anything, Harell! You aren't going anywhere. Do you hear me?"

"Lena, please can you move so I can leave?"

Lena then spat in my face. I stood there, stunned. I couldn't believe what had just happened. To talk to me as if I was worthless was one thing, but to then spit in my face confirming how little she really thought of me was another.

"What are you going to do? What? You want to hit me? Go ahead, hit me! I dare you!" Lena shouted.

Something was truly wrong with her. All of this stemmed from me not wanting to treat her like a sex object, but instead trying to build something with her. I couldn't believe something you would think most women would want could escalate into something like this. I surely knew that if I had realized today would be like this, I would have gone to school instead. At least there, none of this would have happened. Why was I being punished? Why was God putting me through all of this? What had I done to deserve any of it?

Since Lena was blocking my exit, I turned and went to the bathroom and locked the door. I wanted to break down and just cry but I was still in shock. I couldn't believe all that had happened. I calmly washed my face and tried to calm down. I needed to figure out a way to get out of there. Lena wasn't crazy enough to damage John's house so I wasn't worried about that. But it was evident we didn't need to be around each other at that moment.

I noticed I didn't hear the TV anymore, or anything else for that matter. Maybe Lena had done me a favor and decided to leave. I opened the bathroom door and went back into the living room. Unfortunately my guess was wrong. Lena hadn't gone anywhere. All she'd done was turn the TV off and sat back down on the couch. However, she had her head buried in her hands in pity.

"I guess you are going to do what everyone else has and walk out on me, too?" Lena asked.

She lifted her head up and I noticed the tears coming down her face. I was furious, but the minute I saw how much she was in pain, it all subsided.

"Baby, what is going on? What is wrong with you?" I asked.

"Look, it's cool. I know you are going to leave me. I don't blame you. I would leave me, too, if I were you. I'm damaged."

"Baby, I don't want to leave you. I want to be with you, but I also want to help you, and I can't if you don't tell me what is going on."

She got up from the couch and went to grab her book bag.

"It doesn't matter. Just leave me alone!" she responded.

I grabbed her from the back and started to hug her.

"Talk to me, baby. Stop shutting me out!"

"Get off of me, Harell!" Lena screamed.

I didn't even notice John had walked inside the house.

"Get the hell off of me!"

John came and grabbed me.

"Let her go! Go ahead with all that, Harell. It's not worth it."

He didn't know that I wasn't trying to hurt her. I was only trying to get her to talk and tell me what had made her blow up earlier. It was something inside of her deeper than just me.

"I'm cool, John, I swear! We are just talking."

"No, we aren't! I don't have anything left to say to you. I just want to get out of here," Lena said.

"Man, if she wants to go, then go ahead and let her go. Don't try to keep anyone who doesn't want to be kept," John said.

"John, just stay out of this. You don't know what is going on. This is between Lena and me. Please just stay out of it and leave it that way."

"Would you just leave me the HELL ALONE?" Lena yelled and swung at me with something in her hand. It hit me on the side of my face by my right eye. The pain echoed throughout my body.

"Damn it!"

She'd hit me with John's house phone. My next reflex was to swing back. I didn't see a woman. I didn't see Lena. All I saw mentally was a challenge and I needed to defend myself. Thankfully, as I swung in retaliation, John grabbed my arm, stopping it from ever hitting Lena and holding me away from her.

"Lena, you need to get out of my house right now!" John ordered.

Lena did what John asked without hesitation.

"What the hell is wrong with you, Harell? What is going on?"

"I don't know! I don't know! All I wanted to do was talk to her. She had no right to put her hands on me. She spat in my face and then hit me with a telephone. I didn't do anything to that girl!"

I couldn't hold back my emotions any longer. The tears started to stream down my face. This wasn't the first time John had seen me this way and probably wouldn't be the last. I was only seventeen years old but had gone through more in those seventeen years than some men ten years older than me ever had experienced. The miles of road I'd traveled in life finally had my legs tired because I still couldn't see the light at the end of the tunnel. Little did I know that I was still at the beginning of my journey. God had much more in store for me.

CHAPTER 4

UNDERSTANDING EMOTIONAL OR PSYCHOLOGICAL ABUSE

Emotional or psychological abuse can be verbal or nonverbal. Its aim is to chip away at your feelings of self-worth and independence. If you're the victim of emotional abuse, you may feel that there is no way out of the relationship, or that without your abusive partner, you have nothing. Emotional abuse includes verbal abuse such as yelling, name calling, blaming, and shaming. Isolation, intimidation, and controlling behavior also fall under emotional abuse. Additionally, abusers who use emotional or psychological abuse often throw in threats of physical violence.

Each of the three beginning stories all were my exposure to abuse. I experienced abuse on two different levels early on in my childhood, with my first encounter being physical. Usually, this is not the case. Usually, your first encounter is going to be your abuser attacking you mentally.

However, in my case, Stanley was already a seasoned abuser. He knew that in order to attack me mentally, he'd first have to put the fear of physical abuse within me. He couldn't only attack me mentally with verbal abuse and be effective. That wouldn't have worked because mentally I was very strong.

He knew this so he beat me in order to be able to attack me mentally. He knew that every powerful blow he inflicted on my body would leave a more lasting scar on my mind. That was his primary focus.

An abuser's primary mission is dominance or control. Abusive individuals need to feel in charge of the relationship. They will make decisions for you and the family, tell you what to do, and expect you to obey them without question. Even to the degree that an abuser may treat his spouse or partner like a servant, child, or even as his or her possession.

Now you may be under the assumption that physical abuse is far worse than emotional abuse. Physical violence can send you to the hospital and leave you with scars. But, the scars of emotional abuse are very real, and they run much deeper. In fact, emotional abuse can be more damaging than physical abuse. Furthermore, emotional abuse usually worsens over time, often escalating to physical battery.

In my case, the proof was in the pudding. My injuries from being jumped by Dwayne and his friends all healed. Even the bruises placed on my behind by Stanley all healed. However, my mental state never healed. There wasn't a Band-Aid that I could place on my internal wound that would stop the bleeding, so it began to spread within me like a cancer.

Had I never been exposed to abuse, it would have never manifested within me. That is why this is the first stage. The exposure doesn't always have to happen as a child. That happened to be my situation, but it could start with any relationship you are in—whether it be your first, your second, third, or so on. The minute you become exposed to abuse and accept it as acceptable behavior or make excuses for why it happened is when you allow abusive traits to manifest within you.

Look at my first serious relationship. With Lena, it was obvious that her lashings were more than what happened on the surface. It was more than what I knew, but the only way she knew how to react was by verbally abusing me. She tried to make me feel like

I was less of a man because of her insecurities within herself.

It's mirror time. Is this you? Has this happened to you? Do you see yourself in any of the first three stories? If your answer is yes, let's take control of it now before the abuse worsens. Please, seek professional help. You do not have to continue along the path you have started to travel down. This is your life. You can make a detour at any time you chose. Why not now? It's best to try to catch this at the onset versus allowing it to linger and possibly manifest within you. Now I know everyone who is either committing abuse against someone or is being abused by someone isn't going to be privileged enough to catch it at this stage. Each situation is always going to be different, but just as I know this doesn't pertain to everyone, I also know it does to someone. Look at yourself hard in that mirror. Be honest with yourself!

If you are the one who is committing the abuse, I can't stress enough, the fact that you need help. If you ignore my pleas, the abuse will only get worse for both you and your spouse or partner. Emotional abuse can easily turn into domestic violence before you know it. But you first have to want to get help. I'll touch on this more later.

If you are the one who is being abused, you do not have to continue to deal with the emotional and psychological abuse you are being put through. If your partner doesn't want to change his or her ways, please leave. Things will not get better. He or she will not miraculously change overnight. They will have to want to. Once you have made the choice to leave, don't assume that was the final step.

A lot of times when we go through something that hurts us so much, we feel like we would never put another person through the same. However, in reality, this isn't the case. Once you have been exposed to this type of behavior, it can become a part of you without you ever even knowing. Remember right now, you are the one that it's happening to. You are still within the storm. It's not until the storm passes and another storm enters that you know how much damage the first storm caused.

CHAPTER 5

ANGER AND BITTERNESS, THE GOOD AND THE EVIL

A nger isn't always a bad thing. There is nothing wrong with being angry or getting angry. I compare angry with fire. At times, fire will purge and cleanse but it also dies out. The fire never stays lit. You have to do the same with your internal fire. Do not allow the anger within you to continue to burn. It has to die out. If not, your anger will then turn into bitterness.

This is what we don't want. Anger is fine, but bitterness is another story. Bitterness will spread throughout your body like a cancer. I know people who have held on to bitterness for years and years. Forget people, I am one of them. What my mother allowed Stanley to do to me without any repercussions consumed my body. At that point, I lost the childhood innocence every child possesses. I lost all sense of trust because of the one person that I trusted the most ended up hurting me the most. After that point, I couldn't trust anyone because of the bitterness I held onto.

See what usually happens is that bitterness will sit down in you and become a part of you. It's like any other disease that consumes your body. Once it enters your system, if you do not treat it, it will only spread further throughout your body. The longer your body holds onto those bitter feelings, the more likely it will manifest within you. It has to in one way or another.

You cannot continue to hold on to the bitterness from the exposure of abuse or anything else for that matter. Maybe you haven't been exposed to any type of abuse as of yet, however, you are holding on to the pain and bitterness of how a man wronged you in the past. This can cause you to lash out at your new partner and emotionally abuse them for something they had nothing to do with. You have now brought your mental luggage from the past relationship into your current one.

You can't continue to hold on to those types of things. You have to let them go. That doesn't mean go talking to every Tom, Dick, and Harry about your problems either. In other words, don't go telling everyone your business. Just because you look at them as family or friends, doesn't mean that they always have your best interest at heart. They are still human and people tend to give advice based upon what is going on within their lives and have nothing to do with what's going on in yours. And that was the reason you came to them in the first place. So now you are left more confused because you took the advice of someone who was in a worse situation or position than you were.

My suggestion is to call on who loves you most and will never lead you astray and that is Christ. He is still in the healing business and He has been practicing from the start of eternity. Wherever you are right now, get down on your knees and pray. Call out to Him to help you in this situation. Ask Him to give you the strength to take the necessary steps in order to get out of the situation. At the end of the day, you still have to do the work. Prayer alone won't stop what is happening. Action is also needed. But make sure Christ is your first stop. Whenever I'm down, I look to Psalm 62 (NIV) for comfort. It reads:

> *My soul finds rest in God alone; my salvation comes from him.*
> *He alone is my rock and my salvation; he is my fortress, I will never be shaken.*
> *How long will you assault a man?*

Would all of you throw him down—this leaning wall, this tottering fence?

They fully intend to topple him from his lofty place; they take delight in lies.

With their mouths they bless, but in their hearts they curse.

Find rest, O my soul, in God alone; my hope comes from him.

He alone is my rock and my salvation; he is my fortress, I will not be shaken.

My salvation and my honor depend on God; he is my mighty rock, my refuge.

Trust in him at all times, O people; for God is our refuge.

Lowborn men are but a breath, the highborn are but a lie; if weighed on a balance, they are nothing; together they are only a breath.

Do not trust in extortion or take pride in stolen goods; though your riches increase, do not set your heart on them.

One thing God had spoken, two things have I heard; that you, O God, are strong, and that you, O Lord, are loving surely you will reward each person according to what he has done.

It took a long time but I am no longer mad at my mother, or even Stanley, for that matter. Now that I'm grown and I can look back on all that happened, I can see that Stanley didn't know how to love a woman, which then gave my mother the wrong perception of what a man's love should be. What all of this did was influence my perception of what love should be for my future relationships. Once I cried out to Christ, He showed me what love truly is. 1 Corinthians 13:4-13 reads:

Love is patient, love is kind. It does not envy, it does not boast, it is not proud. It is not rude, it is not self-seeking, it is not easily angered, it keeps no record of wrongs. Love does not delight in evil but rejoices with the truth. It always protects, always trusts, always hopes, always preserves.

Love never fails. But where there are prophecies, they will cease; where there are tongues, they will be stilled; where there is knowledge, it will pass away. For we know in part and we prophesy in part, but when perfection comes, the imperfect disappears. When I was a child, I talked like a child, I thought like a child, I reasoned like a child. When I became a man, I put childish ways behind me. Now we see but a poor reflection as in a mirror; then we shall see face to face. Now I know in part; then I shall know fully, even as I am full known.

And now these three remain: faith, hope and love. But the greatest of these is love.

Christ's word allowed me to realize that what I saw wasn't love. What I saw was confusion. After that, I was able to forgive the both of them for the wrong they had committed against me. Yes, that night broke me down to my core but neither my mother nor Stanley, at that time, were on the same level as I was mentally as a child. Because of the disease that filled their bodies, I was far beyond them. For this, there was no reason to be bitter. It was simply a learning experience that I should have taken and used for the better of my life. So yes, I stand here now telling you that I forgive both of them—not because they deserve it, but because I deserve it as well as my own children.

We, as parents, influence our children without their consent or even their knowledge. If you are being abused, or you are abusing someone emotionally, now is the time to clean it up. And please don't dump it onto your children. Our youth have enough obstacles in their paths already without us influencing them negatively even more.

Parents (and this goes for teachers and anybody else who cares for children), you never know who you're raising. Look at the life experiences of people like Barack Obama, Oprah, Tyler Perry and Zane. Each of them had a whole bunch of stuff trying to destroy them, but they didn't allow the world to tear them down. They didn't allow the world to break them, but think how the world would have been affected if their parents had. Would we be better off as a society or worse?

You see, as a parent, you never know who your child is going to grow up to be. But if you don't stop what you are doing, what is evident is the fact that what you hate in yourself will be a part of the child. Your child will end up becoming what you were trying to stop them from becoming in the first place— you or the person who is abusing you.

2nd Stage
MANIFESTATION

THE ACT, PROCESS, OR AN INSTANCE OF MANIFESTING

Manifest

1. Readily perceived by the senses and especially by the sight
2. Easily understood or recognized by the mind

CHAPTER 1

IT'S MY WAY OR NO WAY

I walked into the house, tired from a long day at work. It wasn't easy being nineteen and the head of my household. Lena was still in high school, finishing up her last year. I was footing the bills for our apartment by myself. The second I graduated from high school, I didn't waste any time moving out. I hustled to find a job that paid enough to put things in motion. I lucked up and got a temporary government job. It had the potential to turn into a full-time permanent position but potential was all I needed at the time. I was determined not to continue to live in my mother's house.

My only regret was that I couldn't take my little brother and sister with me. The thought of knowing they would see all that I saw as a child—and maybe even more—scared me. No child should have to endure what I did. But there was nothing that I could do about it. There was no way my mother would allow my brother and sister to live with me. Plus, even if by some miraculous chance she had, I was nowhere near financially or emotionally stable enough to handle that responsibility.

I wished my mother were single and raising them alone. Then there wouldn't be any problem. My mother would break her neck for her children. She did whatever it took to provide for us financially and emotionally. She was simply too blinded by her relationship to see that it also affected us as well. It taught us the wrong perception of what a functional relationship was or should be.

"Hey, baby, how was work?" Lena asked as I walked into the house.

"Long and tiring," I quickly replied before I went over to give her a kiss. "Did you miss me today?"

"Of course I did. When don't I miss you? I know my back and my feet definitely miss you."

"Is that right?"

"Yes! They need to be rubbed ASAP!"

I couldn't help but laugh.

"I'm serious," she reiterated.

"I bet you are. Well, come on over here so I can massage your back and rub those feet of yours. You must have been hardheaded and not taking it easy like you're supposed to be doing."

"Huh?"

"Lena, you know you heard me. Have you been taking it easy? What did the doctor tell you? He specifically said your weight is low and it might be your stress level that is causing it. I need you to take it easy. I don't want my baby coming out with nine toes or something."

Lena was currently six months' pregnant.

"Harell, that is not funny!"

"I'm not trying to be funny, I'm dead serious! I don't want anything happening to you or my baby. I need you to take it easy and relax. For right now, all you really need to be doing is going to class and coming home. That's it. But instead you want to go to pom-pom practice and stuff, like you are still on the squad."

"First of all, I am on the squad. I never left. I just can't compete since I'm pregnant. Now back to your ignorant comment; don't be wishing anything like that on our child."

"Lena, did you hear me say I wish our child has nine toes? No! I'm not wishing anything on our child. Why would I even do something like that? I told you to chill out so nothing like that can happen. I just want you to concentrate on us and our family and stop trying to be superwoman for everyone else."

"Harell, I am fine. I just haven't been eating right is all. Doctor Robinson and I have discussed everything. I have to change my diet and make sure I eat more than what I have been eating. Outside of that, I am fine. I promise, I will get my weight up. The baby will be fine. I will not let anything happen to me or my child but you have to allow me to have a life as well. I am pregnant, I'm not sick. I'm not going to just go to school and then sit around in the house all day. I'm sorry. I'm not going to do that!"

I stopped rubbing her feet and got up off of the couch.

"I guess how I feel doesn't matter. Fine, Lena, do what you want! Just forget I ever said anything since I don't have any say-so in this relationship. You can drive. I'll sit in the passenger seat and mind my business from now on."

"Baby, this is not that serious. Why are you getting all upset? I want you to trust me. I love this child as much as you do. I'm not going to do anything to hurt the baby. Just trust in me, please. I don't want to argue with you. I don't want us to be mad at each other, especially not over this. This is something too small and petty and you know it."

"Man, whatever! Everything that bothers me is something small or I'm always being petty, but the minute it's something that is on your mind; it's supposed to be priority number one. You know what, like I said before, it don't even matter. You are grown; do what you do," I replied.

I walked out of the living room and went into the bedroom. I needed to unwind. Plus, I wanted to get away from Lena. I could feel my emotions starting to get the best of me and I didn't want the matter to escalate. Maybe she was right and I was overreacting. The minute I got in the room, Lena walked in behind me.

"Are you serious? Why are you walking away?" Lena asked.

"Can I change my clothes or do I have to keep my shirt and tie on? Is that okay with you?"

"Now you have an attitude. I can't believe it. Over this crap, wow!" Lena cracked a smirk, then continued, "Fine, have an attitude then. It doesn't even matter anymore. That is your problem. No one can talk to you without you catching an attitude. It's pointless. All I asked you to do is trust in me. Trust that I will not do anything to harm our baby and you can't even do that."

"Lena, I just want to take my damn clothes off. Now who is turning this into something more? It damn sure enough isn't me, so remember that when you start to point the finger at who to blame."

"A minute ago, you weren't thinking about your clothes. Your ass was sitting down on that couch, rubbing my feet like it was nothing. But now you want to go take your clothes off, *after* I ask you to just trust in me. You do this whenever you can't get your way. You are just so selfish. Everything has to be about you."

"What! I ask you to do something for the sake of our child and you have the nerve to call me selfish?" I started to laugh, and then continued, "Yeah whatever! Say what you want. I'm far from damn selfish but I'll tell you this much, this conversation is over. I don't have anything left to say to you."

I turned my back to Lena and before I could sit down, she slammed the bedroom door shut as she left and went back into the living room. I couldn't believe she would call me selfish. All I wanted was what was best for our child. I didn't care what she did. I wanted to make sure the baby was okay. Now if I didn't give a damn about the baby or the pregnancy then I'm insensitive. But because I was trying to do right and be a good dad, I was selfish. It was almost like, why even try. It wasn't going to make any difference. You are damned if you do and damned if you don't.

I lay on the bed, trying to clear my mind. Nothing seemed to help. I wanted to go out in the living room and apologize for whatever my part was in the argument. The house seemed as if it was empty when we were upset with each other. I felt a sense of loneliness. Regardless of how I felt though, my pride wouldn't allow me to apologize. I stayed in the room and figured the best thing to do would be to try to sleep it off. Sooner or later, Lena would try to make up and everything would go back to normal.

The bedroom door opened and Lena walked in.

"Where are the car keys?" she asked.

"Keys for what? What do you need the keys for?"

"Harell, where are the car keys? You don't need to question me about anything. Remember, you don't care what I do anymore so what and why I need the keys should no longer be any of your concern."

"It's my damn car and you are asking me for my keys, so I can be concerned if I want to. Now I'll ask you again, where are you going? What do you need them for?"

"Oh really, it's your car now? That is cool. I'm glad to know that is how you really feel."

"Lena, all I asked is what you need them for? Why are you making every situation so difficult?"

Lena continued to ignore my question. "Just so we are clear on things because we know how you love to try to change things around. Later I don't want you to be like I'm changing what you said around or anything. We know how you are. It's your car, right?"

"Why do you keep asking me the same question over and over again but yet feel the need not to answer mine? Where are you going?"

Lena turned around and walked out of the bedroom. I quickly jumped out of the bed and followed her into the living room. Lena grabbed her purse and was making her way toward the front door. I jumped in front of her so that she couldn't leave.

"Where are you going?"

"Harell, it doesn't even matter. I don't need your car. Can you please move? I have a bus to catch. Shoot, I catch the Metro bus to school every morning, so I can do the same to where I need to go right now since it's *your* car."

"Baby, please, stop! I'm sorry. I didn't mean it like that. Please just tell me where are you trying to go? I'll go get whatever it is you need or take you wherever you need to go."

"I don't need you to do anything for me. Whatever I need, I can get myself."

"Lena, would you please stop!"

"Harell, would you please move!"

We both were at a standstill. Neither of us would budge in our positioning.

"Why are you acting like this? Is this because of earlier? Look, I'm sorry. Shit!"

"You aren't sorry. You just want to control the situation. You always have to control the situation and when you don't get your way, you want to lash out at someone or get in your feelings. I don't know who you have me mixed up with, but I'm not the one! Please believe me, I can do bad all by myself. I don't need you for that."

"Wow, so being with me is bad now? Is that what you're saying?"

"Please don't try to turn or twist my words around. All I want to do is leave so can you please just move so I can go about my business and you yours?"

"No, we are going to sit down and talk about this," I replied.

"There you go, trying to control the situation again. When you didn't want to talk and wanted to take your clothes off, did I jump in front of you? No, I let you pout and take your ass in the room and do whatever it was you needed to do. Right now I need to get out of this house. You've already said that I cannot use *your* car, so can you please move so I can catch the damn bus?"

"Okay, fine. Can you tell me where you're going and I'll move?"

"No, because what I need to do or where I'm going is none of your damn business. Again, I am grown and can go wherever I please."

I sighed. I didn't know what else to do.

"I'm not moving so I don't know what to tell you."

Frustrated, Lena swung at me. The punch missed and I quickly grabbed a hold of her.

"Baby, please stop!" I said, holding her.

"Why won't you let me leave? I want to go. You don't want to be bothered with me, so I don't want to be bothered with you. You can not control me. You are not my father, Harell."

"I don't want to be your father. I want to be your husband one day. Come on; let's just sit down and talk."

"I said I don't want to talk to you. I want to leave. You always want to talk on your time or when it's convenient to you. I'm sorry but it doesn't work that way. This is a relationship. It's not always about Harell. I'm in this relationship, too. I have feelings also. You got mad because I chose to go to pom-pom practice. It's not like I'm going to the club or something like that, or putting our child in jeopardy. I don't want to be stuck up in this house twenty-four/seven. Would you want to be? No! Instead of listening to what I was telling you, you catch an attitude because I wasn't doing what you wanted or saying what you wanted to hear. I have nothing to say to you; nothing at all!"

"Lena, I'm sorry. I really am. You are right! You are right about everything! I apologize."

I held onto her tightly, hugging her. I could feel Lena starting to give in, and then she pulled away.

"No, stop! Let me go," she said.

"I can't. I won't. I love you too much!"

I continued to hold onto her. I wouldn't let her go. I wanted her to feel and know that I was there for her. I wasn't going to allow her to run from every problem we had. We could work through anything. That is what love is.

"If you really love me, then you would move so I can leave. Please, Harell, just let me leave. That is all I'm asking."

"Why do you always have to run? Why can't we work it out?"

"STOP TRYING TO CONTROL ME! Move so I can go, please. YOU ARE NOT MY FATHER!" Lena yelled.

"Fine, Lena, here take the keys," I said as I placed them in her hands.

Lena threw the keys on the floor.

"I don't want to use *your* car. I just want to leave!"

"Please, take the car. I hate it when you are on the bus. It's rough out in these streets. Please, take the car. It's our car. Everything in this house is ours. *We* share everything. There is nothing that is mine and vice versa. We are a family. We are one."

"Whatever... just give me the damn keys so I can leave!"

I picked the keys up from off of the floor and handed them to her. Lena didn't even look twice at me. All she did was head out the door and made sure to slam it shut.

CHAPTER 2

I'M GOING OUT TONIGHT

Times were hard for Lena. After she had the baby, she wasn't able to find employment. It wasn't in Lena to sit around anyone's house and be a housewife; especially when we weren't even married. She was nothing more than a baby's mother who had no job; that she hated. She didn't hide her frustrations with that either.

After a while, I developed the skill to ignore her. It wasn't as if I was trying to be mean or insensitive. I needed to understand that her frustrations weren't with me but rather with the situation. If she started to bicker or argue, I would let her get whatever it was off of her chest. As soon as she did, it escaped my ears.

Occasionally, I would try to fight her negativity by encouraging her and letting her know everything would work out for the better. If she continued to look for employment, eventually she'd get a job. In actuality, though, her unemployment didn't bother me. I actually preferred it that way. We weren't struggling with money. I was making enough to handle our bills, and I felt comfortable with her at home with our son. I didn't have to worry about him being at day care with a stranger and adding another bill to our stack.

Of course Lena and I didn't see eye to eye about that and I understood why. She wanted to be able to contribute to society as well. At times I felt bad for her, but the majority of the time I didn't. I know it was a selfish way to think, but I couldn't help it.

Regardless of my feelings, I tried to never push her one way or the other. I tried my best to stay neutral about the situation. It was bad enough she thought I was trying to control her. I definitely didn't want this one added onto my stockpile.

The phone started ringing, breaking Lena out of her daily depression.

"Hello," Lena answered.

"Hey, girl, what are you doing?" her girlfriend Maxine asked.

"Nothing much; just put Tre down to sleep and now sitting here watching a little TV."

"Where is Harell?"

"He hasn't gotten in from work yet. He should be in here shortly, though."

"Well, guess what? I heard we are about to have some openings at the post office. I'm pretty sure I can get you at least an interview, if not the job. All you need to do is apply and make sure you represent me right."

"Are you serious? Child, if you can pull that off, I'd be so thankful. I'm going out of my mind sitting around this house. I only thought it would be for the first six weeks after I had him, but that quickly turned into six months. There are only but so many daytime soaps a person can watch."

Maxine started laughing. "I know that's right. Yeah, my supervisor asked me earlier today if I knew anyone who was looking for work because of the openings. So you know I told her I did. She is the one who told me to tell you they'll be posting the job either next week or the week after. She really isn't sure of the exact day, but she said make sure you check next Tuesday or the following Tuesday. Once you apply, let me know and she'll look out for your name and schedule your interview and everything."

"Cool...that sounds perfect. I know Harell probably will be in his feelings, but he'll get over it."

"Huh, why do you say that? You would think he would be happy you found a job. I know handling everything around there has to be taking its toll on him."

"Yeah right, he couldn't care less. He probably wants it that way. You should hear him. He throws his little hints out there all the time. He'll say he doesn't trust Tre with just anyone or how maybe this is God's way of showing me He doesn't want me working right now, and I should be home with Tre. That boy will say anything these days."

"You are kidding me? Are you serious? Not God don't want you working, though. Wow, I really didn't think he was like that. I figured Harell would jump at the chance of you working. Shoot, formula isn't cheap these days and neither are diapers."

"I know but he feels like he can handle everything. Just put it on his shoulders and it's done. It don't matter what it is. He can take it all on. He is always giving money to his little sister every chance she needs it, then he makes sure I have money in my pocket. He acts like we living large or something when I know we aren't. I know how much he makes. I know what the bills are and so forth. I don't know what is wrong with that boy. I'm not stupid, though. He thinks I don't know he is out in these streets making money also. I can add and the money we have coming in with what should be coming in isn't adding up. Extra money is included."

"No, not Harell," Maxine replied.

"Yes, Harell. I haven't called him out on it because I knew he was only trying to do for us and his family, but if I'm working, he can stop all that. I don't want my son to grow up with his father in jail. It's like he tries to carry the burden of the world on his back. He doesn't know how to only handle what he can handle and put the rest by the wayside. No, he has to be Captain America and save everyone. I will never understand why. I mean, I know he loves his little sister and all but…never mind, I'm not even going to go there."

"But what makes you think he is in the street? Is he bringing it home or something?"

"No, nothing like that. I just know. I can tell. Remember my brother was in the streets before he got locked up on the cocaine charge. I remember folks knocking on the door looking for him, trying to cop whatever drug it was he was selling at the time. He always had money but yet had no job. I remember all of that. It's the same with Harell. I see his pay stubs. I know how much our rent is. I know how much the cable and telephone bill are.

"Once he pays all that of his paycheck, you should have maybe two to three hundred to spare a month. That's not factoring in you getting gas for the car, food for the house, diapers, formula and stuff for Tre. But yet you still giving me a hundred a week for me to get my hair done, nails done, or anything else I want. Then it's not like you not shopping for yourself or giving your sister money or food for their house or whatever else. Come on, Maxine, do the math."

"Yeah, I guess you do have a point. I just never figured Harell to be that type of man. I mean, I knew he would do whatever is necessary to take care of his family, but he never seemed like that. What are you going to do? Are you going to talk to him about it?"

"I doubt it. For what? Especially if I get the job, there is no need to. The way I see it, he'll stop because now I'm bringing in money to help with bills. Plus, we argue about enough as it is and honestly, I don't even feel like running the risk of him lying to me and making matters worse. It's just best if I leave it alone and let it blow in the wind."

"Dag, girl, yeah, I see why you are so depressed up in there. Well, I have just the thing to cheer you up. I don't have to work tomorrow, so let's go out tonight and hit the Mirage."

"I don't know. I haven't been out in a while," Lena responded.

"Exactly, that is why you need to get out. You are in that house enough. When Harell come home, just tell him you are going out tonight. Girl, you never go out. I'm sure he knows that. You need to get out! Come on!"

I walked into the house. Lena continued her conversation.

"Yeah, I guess you are right."

"I know I'm right; you know I'm right. I'll be there a little after nine p.m. to pick you up."

"I don't recall saying I was going yet. All I said was that I guess you are right. Nowhere in there did I say, I'm going."

"Whatever, Lena, make sure your butt is ready by nine. You know how it takes you forever and a day to get ready."

"Yeah, okay, I'll think about it," Lena said and started to laugh.

"I got some errands to run real quick before I head home to get ready myself. Chick, please be ready when I get there. I'm really not trying to have to come inside when I get there."

"Why, what's wrong?"

"Don't try to act brand new. You know Harell can't stand me. I'm far from in the mood to deal with his little attitude tonight."

"Girl, please, bye!"

"I'm serious, chick. Be ready by nine."

"Yeah, yeah, yeah… Bye!"

They both hung up the phone.

Lena got up off of the couch and came over to greet me when I arrived.

"Hey, baby. How was work today?" she asked as she planted a soft kiss on my lips.

"Not bad. I think they are finally going to bring me on full-time and remove the temporary detail tag from my title."

"That's good. I know you are happy about that."

"Why wouldn't I be? That way I finally get benefits like a regular full-time government employee and have insurance. I can finally take Tre off your mom's insurance and put him on mine, and also I'd get a grade increase. We can definitely use the extra money and get out of this apartment and get a better one."

"Why, what's wrong with where we live? Why not use the extra money to get a new car instead, so that way we have two cars?"

"Baby, I can't handle a car note right now. We are just maintaining our bills now. Why add an extra one to it? It would be different if you were working and we had two incomes coming into the house; then, yeah, we possibly could do something like that. But right now, I think if we are going to have a monthly increase, it should be because we moved into a new apartment in a better neighborhood. I don't want my son to grow up like you and I did."

"I understand, baby, and I love you for that. But back to something you said about me working...I think I'm finally going to break through and get a job."

"Oh really, why do you say that?"

"I was just on the phone with Max and she said that her supervisor told her they will be posting a new position opening either next week or the week after. Max will let me know when they post it. She said she can definitely get me an interview. That's all I need. I know how to sell myself so I'm not worried. I just needed an interview."

"At the post office? I thought you wanted to dance. Those two don't go hand in hand. Working at the post office will not land you on a Broadway stage dancing. What happened to you going back to school?"

"We have a family and that's my top priority. The bottom line is I need a job. I'm not going to get any auditions while in Maryland regardless. And we have no money for me to travel to New York for auditions, so that is the farthest thing from my mind right now. That was a childhood dream before I ended up pregnant and had a family that I needed to help support."

"We are above water right now. You can go back to school and major in dance. I can keep us afloat while you do so."

"Harell, did you not say just two minutes ago how things would be different if I was working, and we'd be able to get another car since I'd be helping financially around here? Now you are telling me we are afloat and go back to school. You aren't making any sense. Well, actually you are. You are making perfectly good sense. Why don't you tell me how you really feel? You don't want me to work. Why not say that instead of sugarcoating it? Either way, it doesn't matter how you feel because I'm going to apply, I'm going to go on the interview, and I'm going to get the job regardless of how you feel. I'm not going to be a housewife to a man whom I'm not even married to."

"Is that what this is all about, marriage? You want to go and get married or something, baby?"

"No, that is not what this is about. I want to get a job. I need to do something with my life. I didn't go to school to stay at home. Some women might love being able to stay at home and take care of the kids, but I am not one of them. I want a job."

"Okay, baby, that is fine. If that is what you want to do, then I'll support you. Okay?"

"Thank you!"

"No problem…so where are you going?"

"Huh, what are you talking about?"

"I heard you say on the phone you were going somewhere."

"Oh, yeah, I'm going out tonight," she replied.

"Oh really, with who?"

"Max, who else?"

"Oh, okay," I said and walked into the room. I didn't want her to know that I was upset, even though I was. I couldn't believe she was going out with Maxine, of all people. Maxine had no respect for men. Lena would gossip and tell me on a constant basis how much Maxine played guys. She would use them for money or whatever else as long as she benefited. She had no problem using sex as a weapon as well. I hated the fact that they were friends, but there was nothing I could do about it. I had to find the right way to go about this. There was no way she was going out with Maxine.

Lena walked into the bedroom and started to iron her clothes.

"So where are y'all going tonight?"

"Max wants to go to the Mirage," she replied.

"I thought you didn't like to go to clubs?"

"I don't. They aren't really my cup of tea but why not. I need to get out and have a little fun. I haven't been out in I don't know how long. All I do is stay home with you and Tre. I mean, there is nothing wrong with that, but I never get out and have any *me* time. You get to go out and hang out with John all the time. I need to get out every now and then also."

"I get that…but to a nightclub and with Maxine, I don't know about that."

"What is that supposed to mean?"

"What?"

"*And with Maxine*, what is that supposed to mean?"

"You know exactly what it means. Don't try to act brand new. You tell me how she is with men. I know what her purpose is for going out. It's to meet guys and whatever. Why would you want to be around someone like that? You know what they say; all birds of a feather flock together."

"I am a grown woman. What another woman does has nothing to do with me. Just because she talks to guys or whatever the case may be, doesn't mean I am. I am with you and regardless of who I go out with, you should trust me enough to know that I would never disrespect you or this relationship. You make it seem like Max be trying to get me to talk to guys or something and, even if she did, that I would. You and I have a family together. We have a child together. Why would I do that?"

"People cheat every day, all day, and they have families. They are married and even more so, what does that have to do with anything?"

"Why don't you just say you don't trust me? I'd respect you more if you were honest about your feelings, instead of trying to make this about Max."

"You're so quick to tell me not to put words into your mouth, but yet you are constantly putting them into mine. I never said I don't trust you. I don't trust her and I definitely don't trust the niggas at the clubs. I know what their intentions are."

"Okay, but no one can do anything I don't let them do. You have to trust me to not hurt you. I don't want anyone else. I just want to go out and have fun. I have been cooped up in this house for far too long. This has nothing to do with a man or meeting a man. We could be going to IHOP for all I care. I want to get out of the house. It just so happens she wanted to go to the Mirage and I agreed."

"Fine, forget it. Do what you want to do. How I feel doesn't matter. I ask you not to hang with her and it's screw how I feel. I'm not your man. I'm not your partner. I'm just the guy you live with. You don't respect my feelings or my opinion."

"Don't try to turn this around on me. You know that is far from the truth. Max was my friend before you and will be my friend after you. I wish you would respect that and stop trying to change everything about me."

"I'm not trying to change you and I wish you would stop saying that. Damn!"

"You are! You don't want me hanging with this person. You don't want me doing that. What the hell do you want me to do? I mean, what is acceptable? Then you tried to make it about the club. If I called Max up right now and said let's go see a movie and have dinner, would that make you feel better?"

"No, I don't want you hanging with her. I already told you that."

"Exactly, so this has nothing to do with me going to the club. She is my friend and regardless of what you want, I'm going out with her. You are going to have to deal with that."

"What?"

"You heard me, Harell. I'm not staying in this house tonight. I am going out with Max tonight. Now I have to take my shower. I'll finish ironing my clothes when I get out."

Lena walked out of the room and went into the bathroom to take her shower. I couldn't believe she was still going to go out even after I told her not to. It was obvious she didn't respect me or my wishes. All she cared about was Maxine. I quickly changed my clothes while Lena was in the shower, grabbed my car keys and headed out the door. She couldn't go anywhere if I wasn't home because someone had to watch Tre. I didn't care if she got mad, either. She would get over it. I didn't want her going out with Maxine and this was the only solution I could think of.

CHAPTER 3

YOUR MONEY IS YOURS AND MINE IS MINE

It seemed like the more money we made, the more bills would pile up. I couldn't understand it. How did things go from me being able to maintain everything when Lena wasn't working, to now, where everything but rent seemed like it was a month or two behind? Even though I was no longer in the streets hustling, it still shouldn't have made a difference with Lena now working. The post office paid damn good money. There was no way we should've been as behind as we were, with both of our incomes. I had even received several step increases throughout the years, I was making way more money from the Department of Health and Human Services.

It wasn't as if our bills drastically increased. We only added two extra expenses: day care and a car note. I went ahead and agreed to get a new car the minute Lena was offered the job at the post office. I didn't want to get the car. However, Lena had a very good point: We needed a new car. This was 2001 and I was still driving around in a 1985 Dodge Aries. Who knew when that car would give out and finally die? We needed something reliable and dependable, especially with us being on child number four now.

I guess that should have answered why everything increased. I walked into the house and started my daily routine. I opened the bills and held my breath. It was funny how quickly you could go from one month behind to three, and facing disconnection. My house phone and my cable both were in jeopardy of being cut off, and the electric wasn't too far behind.

Times were definitely hard and my faith was running extremely low. It seemed like every time I would get a handle on things, Lena would do something stupid with her money. We'd end up right back in the same hole we'd just climbed out of. She was always loaning her mother money or whatever the case would be. I know I took care of my little sister and gave her a few dollars here and there, but she was my baby sister. This was her mother, a grown woman. Plus, I never gave my sister money that I didn't have. At the time, I had extra bread and could spare it. Lena didn't. How do you loan someone money you don't even have? Where do they do that?

As much as I didn't want to, my next step was going to be getting back out there on that block and grinding for the quick dollar. I didn't want to run the risk of getting locked up but what choice did I really have? I wasn't due for another increase for close to five months and even that wasn't guaranteed. I could've always tried to find another job, but most employers weren't beating down the door to offer more money to a twenty-four-year-old black man with no college degree.

Lena walked into the house with the kids. I saw she was struggling, so I put what I had in my hands down and went over to the door to give her a hand.

"Thank you! Can you take them in the house? I have to go back outside and get the rest of the bags."

"Baby, we are already in the house," I said, laughing. "Go get your bags."

Tre was now six years old. We also had RaShawn and Malik, who were both four years old and our baby girl, Yhanae, who was barely six months old.

"Hi, Daddy," the boys said.

"Hey, fellas. How was school?"

"We went outside and played and had string beans for lunch," RaShawn said.

I couldn't help but laugh. Things were so much simpler when you were a child. If you could only go back in time was what I often thought, but that wasn't an option.

"Is that right, Shawn? What about you, Tre? How was school?"

"Okay, I guess. We didn't do much today."

"Why is that?"

"I don't know. We just didn't."

"Okay, well, do you have any homework? Let me see your book bag."

"Here, Dad," Malik said. "Here is mine."

"Thanks, little man!"

I took all their book bags and went into the bedroom with Yhanae. I needed to take off her coat and stuff. I knew she was getting hot. Thankfully, she was still asleep. That wouldn't last long, though. Lena walked into the room with bags from Nordstrom and Macy's.

"What is that? I hope there's formula or something in those bags."

"No, I told you my mother is going to watch the kids, and I am going out with Max this weekend?"

"Okay, but what does that have to do with those bags?"

"I had to go shopping. What do I look like, wearing the old stuff in my closet?"

"You look like anyone else who does. Lena, we are struggling enough as it is. The cable and the phone are about to get turned off, and you out shopping to go tricking with some damn Maxine."

"I'm going to ignore your little tricking comment. As for the bills, why haven't you paid them yet? Don't try to turn this around on me. Those are your bills. I have day care and part of rent. Those are the bills that I am responsible for."

"Have you forgotten that you haven't paid your part of the rent in the last three months? Every time the first of the month rolls around, you tell me you are going to give it to me on your next check and I never see it. I have been footing everything around here. You haven't bought groceries. All you do is shop and give your damn mother money."

"Hold on, why are you clocking what I do with my funds? You don't see me tracking down every dime you spend. Where is all your money going? Didn't you just say that the cable and phone are about to get turned off? Why is that? What are you spending your money on?"

"Nothing, my money can't go anywhere because I have to cover what you don't do around here. This is getting ridiculous. Where did you even get money from to buy this stuff? You don't get paid until next Friday and I know you don't have anything saved up."

"I took it out the joint account. I'll put it back in next week when I get paid."

"You did what?"

"You heard me. I used the joint account."

"Lena, the money in there is for rent. Hello, it's the beginning of the month. I just dropped off the rent check this morning. So you mean to tell me our rent check is going to bounce because you wanted to go shopping for an outfit so you can go out this weekend? Please tell me I'm dreaming. I know that is not what you just did."

"Why would you write the check without telling me? How was I supposed to know you were going to pay the rent today?"

"Today is the damn fourth. It's due the fifth of every month. When did you think I was going to write it? Tomorrow? Even if you thought that, you talking about you are going to put it back in there *next* Friday. What you think? The rental office is going to hold the check?"

"No, I didn't say all of that. Well, I don't know what you are going to do because I can't take it back."

"What! I don't give a damn about you going out. If you not taking that crap back, I will. I'll be damned if the rent check bounces because you wanted to act like something you not. You like to lend money so much, go borrow the money to shop with from your mom for all I care. All I know is whatever is in them bags is going back and the money put back into the account. I don't care if you do it or me, but either way it's going back."

"Whatever, Harell. I said how I felt and that is that. Just pay the thirty-five-dollar return check fee and pay the rent once I put it in the joint account next week. It's not a big deal."

"Do you understand we live here? This is where we live. Why would you jeopardize your home for an outfit to wear to the club? I mean, come on. You have plenty of outfits that you can wear. If you don't want to rock any of them, then maybe you don't need to be going out."

"So that is what this is all about. You don't want me to go out," she responded.

"Man, in all honesty, I don't care what you do. Go out and stay out for all I care. You don't have to come back if you don't want to."

The pain from my words showed on Lena's face.

"Is that right? So you want me to move out, Harell? Is that what you are saying?"

I calmed myself down because I was speaking purely off anger and not my true feelings. She had me so upset by her actions that I was reacting without thinking.

"No, that's not what I want. I want you to be more responsible with our bills and our household."

"So now I'm not responsible?"

"No, you aren't responsible. Your actions today show how irresponsible you really are. You are willing to risk us possibly getting evicted all because you want to buy an outfit to go to the club. That isn't responsible. Even if it didn't affect rent, we are behind on our bills. The responsible thing would have been for you to say here, let's use this for the cable or the phone or go out and stock up on diapers and formula. I mean, anything. You could have even gone shopping for the kids. They need clothes more than you and I do. Those were all responsible things to do, if you had extra money."

Lena knew she was wrong. Her lack of a response was all the evidence needed. She always had a reply for every situation. I stood there, trying to think of the best solution. I'd just dropped the check off at the rental office earlier in the day so more than likely they'd submit it to their bank tomorrow. And it would hit mine by Monday with the weekend coming. In other words, I needed to put whatever money she took out back in the joint account by tomorrow morning to be on the safe side.

"How much did you take out?"

Lena hesitated.

"How much?" I asked again.

"Three hundred," she replied.

I couldn't believe it. I walked out of the bedroom and into the living room. The boys were sitting down on the floor watching cartoons. Lena was right behind me.

"Harell, please come back in the room so we can finish talking."

"Lena, right now I don't have anything to say to you. That is almost half our rent and for something to wear tonight? Yeah right!"

"Harell, not in front of the boys," she pleaded.

I looked down and all three of them were staring at me with their big eyes, listening to our conversation.

"I need to get out of here. Don't worry about the money next week. Don't worry about anything. It's obvious I can't rely on you. It's obvious you don't give a damn about this family or what is going on in this house. You are in your own little world. That is cool, though. I will take care of everything. I don't need you to do anything. I know how to grind. I know how to get the bread I need. You keep tricking out in these streets with Max. That is all that matters to you."

"Baby, please, can we just talk about this?"

"Talk about what, Lena? About what? I mean really, we never talk. You say what you want to, I say what I want to, and that is that."

"Please, come into the bedroom and let's talk," she pleaded.

Reluctantly, I agreed and followed her into the bedroom. I was wrong for saying all that I had in front of the boys. Yhanae was different; she was only six months and didn't understand a word either of us was saying. However, the boys definitely did.

"What's up, what do you want to talk about? I've said all I need to say," I said the minute Lena closed the door.

"I'm sorry. I really am. I wasn't thinking. I'll take the stuff back."

"Lena, this isn't the first time. You do this all the time. All that matters to you is Lena. I know you love me and the kids, but you doing what is best for us is nowhere in your mind. You want to be selfish and concentrate solely on Lena, and that isn't fair to me or those kids."

Lena had no reply.

"It's cool, though. Keep your little outfits and boots or whatever you spent the three hundred on. I'll get out here in these streets and get that money back. I'll be damned if I allow you or anyone to have me and our kids homeless and out on the street. If I pay nothing else, I'll make sure that rent is paid."

"No, Harell, I don't want you to do that. What happens if you get caught and locked up?"

"*Now* that matters to you? Why? Since when? You haven't been concerned about my well-being in the past. Why now?"

"I'm always concerned about your well-being. Stop saying that," she replied.

"Whatever! Like I said, I'll take care of everything and I will definitely call the bank after the check clears and cancel the joint account. From now on, your money is your money and mine is mine!"

CHAPTER 4

TOTAL CONTROL

D o you know the primary focus of an abusive person? His or her main goal is to control the person they are in a relationship with. Many tactics will be used to achieve this objective. The four I'm going to concentrate on include dominance, humiliation, isolation and intimidation. It's that time again. It's mirror time. Let's go, ladies and gentlemen. If you are on the couch reading this book or lying in the bed, get up and go find your mirror. It's time to look at yourself in it. After reading each tactic, ask yourself, is this me?

DOMINANCE

Abusive individuals need to feel in charge of the relationship. They will try to make decisions for you and the family, tell you what to do, and expect you to obey without question. An abuser may treat you like a servant, child, or even as their possession.

Man, I hate the phrase "head of household." You see, I presumed being the head of my household meant that I was supposed to make the decisions. I had the final say. That isn't what being the head of a household is. Ladies, this goes for you, too. This isn't directed toward only men. This is the twenty-first century, and it's not uncommon for a woman to make more money than her man these days.

Just because you bring in the majority of the money, you are in a relationship or marriage. Those are unions. You are in a partnership, not a dictatorship. My problem was I was quick to say what my partner could and couldn't do. I thought it was my right to dictate. Or I would make excuses for my actions, which led me to believe I wasn't doing anything wrong. "I don't like her so I don't want you hanging with her" or "Why are you wearing that small skirt?" or "Where have you been?" These were statements I found myself making to my partner all the time. I wanted to control her and not allow her to be my partner. Is this you?

HUMILIATION

An abusive person will do everything he or she can to make you feel badly about yourself, or defective in some way. After all, if you believe you're worthless and that no one else will want you, you're less likely to leave. Insults, name-calling, shaming, and public put-downs are all weapons of abuse designed to erode your self-esteem and make you feel powerless.

I would be a rich man right now if I had a dollar for every time I heard a man or woman tell their spouse or partner that they'd never find another person to treat them better than they do. The reality of it is, that is all a bunch of crap. What they are really saying is I don't want you to go searching for someone else who WILL treat you better than I do. They have to remove any thought of you leaving them.

Remember, I use my life to help yours. I recall one situation where I was dating a gem—a very good woman who had all the qualities a man would want. However, I wasn't ready for the type of commitment she desired or needed. At the same time, I didn't want to leave the door open for her to find it elsewhere. I figured one day I'd be ready and when I was, I needed her there waiting for me. When time started to weigh on her and she realized the game I was playing, I tried to use humiliation to control her and the situation. I told her no man would want to be with a woman who had two children by two different men. Who would want that headache or that drama? That was bull, because if that was the case, then why did I want her? I didn't care about her past but only the future the two of us could build together when I was ready for that step. But I played on her low self-esteem to control her. Is this you?

ISOLATION

In order to increase your dependence on him, an abusive partner will cut you off from the outside world. He may keep you from seeing family or friends, or even prevent you from going to work or school. You may have to ask permission to do anything, go anywhere, or see anyone.

I hated whenever my woman went out. I was very insecure. One reason for my insecurity was my prior ways as a man-whore who would screw anything that walked. I knew how men thought. No man goes to the club trying to find a wife. He is looking for quick fun—a woman who has no problem with a no-strings-attached agreement or one who is having problems in a relationship and needs to blow off steam. Or a drunk who he can try to take advantage of, then put them in a situation where he'll get what he wants.

Now all men aren't the same; some do go to the club just to get out but, again, they aren't going to find a wife. The ones who are looking for quick fun couldn't care less if you have a man. I know this because I couldn't have cared less. In most situations, I preferred you did have a man. It made the situation less of a headache for me after we were done. Remember sex is the main objective, not a relationship.

What did I try to do to avoid my woman from wanting to go out? I isolated her. I always wanted her at home or if she needed to go out, it was with me. I hated her friends. Though some were bad for her, most weren't, but it didn't matter. The fact that she was going out with them was what I hated the most because it was an opportunity for another man to do to me what I'd done to so many other men who were in relationships. Is this you?

INTIMIDATION

An abusive person may use a variety of intimidation methods designed to scare you into submission. These include making threatening looks or gestures, smashing things in front of you, destroying property, hurting your pets, punching walls, or putting weapons on display. The clear message is that if you don't obey, there will be violent consequences. Threats are also another form of intimidation. An abuser commonly uses threats to keep his or her victim from leaving. Your abuser might threaten to hurt or kill you, your children, other family members, or even pets. He or she may also threaten to commit suicide, file false charges against you, or report you to Child Services.

I can't count how many times I thought I had broken my hand from hitting the wall. I can't count how many holes I have punched into a wall, all to gain my woman's attention. My intention was never to put my hands on her; it was merely to show her how frustrated I was and hoped that she would stop making me feel that way. I couldn't see that she didn't control my frustration. I did. There should never be a time when you get to a point where you feel the need to destroy something. If you are this frustrated, sooner or later you are going to explode. How many times have you said, "I can't live without you," or tried to fake suicide when your partner wants to move on with his or her life? This is all a form of intimidation, designed to try to control your partner and the situation.

Again I ask, is this you? Now I need you be honest with yourself. Don't make excuses or say I do this because of that. It's a simple yes-or-no question. Remember, my purpose is not to judge you. My purpose is only to cast a light on the warning signs I ignored that showed the exposure I had with abuse were manifesting within me. I don't want you to make that same mistake. No one is perfect. We are all flawed. Life is about striving for perfection and not continuing to live within our imperfections. Each day I strive to be better than I was the day prior. Won't you join me? Take a good hard look in that mirror. A very good one!

If you are being abused or feel that you are, this is section is for you. A person dealing with a spouse or partner with controlling behavior can leave them with feelings of resentment, depression, and low self-esteem. It also tears at the fabric of a relationship and corrodes every aspect of married life, from finances to social life to sex life. While the controlling partner acts out because of emotional conditioning from their childhood or a past relationship, his or her partner needs to look at their role as an enhancer. Remember, your partner might not see the symptoms of the past manifesting in them. However, you can. You can see their controlling traits so you are in a position to put an end to it; especially if it's caught early and not continued throughout your relationship.

1. Identify the frequency and depth of the controlling partner's behavior. If it occurs in one area of the relationship, it will be easier to discuss and eliminate. I still feel therapy is needed as a tool to discover how the controlling issues initially manifested within your partner. Now if the controlling spouse or partner tries to keep his or her partner from different life aspects, such as friendships, hobbies and work, therapy is a must. Discussing it will not eliminate the issue. This is whether you want to stay in the rela-

tionship and want things to work out between the two of you or
not. Keep in mind you have now been exposed to abuse. It is
possible that it will manifest within you. Don't think that leaving
will solve your issue. Continue to seek help so you can totally
move forward.

2. Refuse to accept the controlling behavior or enable it. Once you
realize that your spouse's or partner's controlling behavior is a
result of his or her emotional problems, you will begin to feel
stronger and work toward improving the situation. Caving in to
their controlling behavior and anger only makes things worse.
Ironically, when you "obey" a controlling person, it gives them
more power, and they seek to control you even more.

3. Consult a therapist. Remember that controlling spouses and
partners act this way because of deep-rooted anger, usually
because of cruel or angry parents, a difficult childhood, or a previous relationship. Do not see their actions as your fault. The
problem stemmed from before they met you. If they won't consent
to seeing a counselor, temporary or permanent withdrawal from
the relationship needs to be your next option. Matters are not
likely to get better, but instead worse. Before a person can bring
change into their life, they have to want to change first.

**4. Repair any emotional damage that the controlling spouse or partner
has inflicted upon you.** As I said in Step 1, this is your exposure to
abuse. Just as your partner was exposed to this behavior and
deemed it acceptable, so too it can happen to you. The only way
you can avoid it from manifesting within you, is to deal with it at
the onset. Work on renewing your own power and interests, and
discard any fearful notions your spouse placed in your psyche. If
your partner doesn't want to talk to a counselor or therapist, take
this time to do so yourself. Before you can love anyone else, you
must first love yourself.

5. Work on changing the marriage or relationship. This is the last step for a reason. It's by design. When a person wants to change, most of the time it's for the wrong reason. Change can help your relationship or marriage, but don't let your relationship or marriage be the only reason for the change. Now, if this is understood, this takes effort from both partners. The controlling person has to dedicate themselves to shedding old angers and fears, and their partner needs to remain strong and not succumb to unjust demands for fear of losing their partner or retaliation from them. Enough said!

IN EVERY SITUATION THAT I WITNESSED AS A CHILD BETWEEN STANLEY AND MY MOTHER, IT DEALT WITH CONTROL. This was from both my mother and Stanley. Stanley's focus was to try to establish control over my mother and within their relationship. My mother was trying to keep the control she had over herself and not relinquish it to him. That was their struggle. Even though this is what I saw my mother and Stanley experience during my childhood, I never saw that it had manifested within me and that I was doing the same thing within my own relationship.

In each of the three stories told in this stage, I illustrated examples of how I tried to control Lena and her actions. If they didn't meet up with my expectations, then they were wrong and either I had an attitude or I did things to get my way. I tried to control who she was friends with. I tried to control where she went. In essence, I wanted to control her life.

That isn't a relationship. That isn't a union or a bond. But in my eyes and in my mind that was my perception of what a relationship should be because that was all I saw. Though I hated Stanley for everything he did to my mother and the way he treated her, his ways had manifested within me without me ever knowing or realizing it.

When Lena wanted to go out with Maxine and nothing I said worked to get her to change her mind, I did the one thing I could think of to control the situation. I left and went out while she was in the shower. There was no way she could go anywhere with an infant child, no car, and no baby sitter. She had to call Maxine and cancel their plans. Never did I think of how Lena was feeling. She even tried to explain how she felt being cooped up in the house, but it never registered. Better yet, I didn't want to listen. My main concern was Maxine and how she lived her life. That scared me because I thought since Maxine lived that way, Lena would want to, the more she hung with her. In my mind, my actions were right. I felt that she didn't need to be with Maxine. And the more Lena fought me on it, I didn't see it as her simply needing to get out of the house or her feeling confined or imprisoned within her own home. I saw it as her being defiant.

I looked at Lena as a child. Usually a child is what when they are up to no good: defiant. That is how I saw Lena. But Lena wasn't a child. She was my partner. She was my spouse, my mate, and my companion, yet I looked at her as a child. I didn't have any faith in the relationship we had built. But how could I when we didn't build a healthy relationship to begin with? What did I have to have faith in? Nothing! And subconsciously, I already knew this. Insecurity is a demon like no other. There was a lot in my past, so I was very insecure about Lena leaving me. I feared that Lena was too good for me. I feared that I was inadequate. If Lena interacted with other men, she would find one better than me, and she would be gone in an instant.

Prior to Lena, that was all I was used to. I was used to being the nice guy. I was the good friend, but because I was sensitive, I was viewed as a weak man. Therefore, I was fearful and that fear heightened my controlling behavior. I had no self discipline within myself. In 2 Timothy 1:1-7 (NIV) it reads:

> *I thank God, whom I serve, as my forefathers did, with a clear conscience, as night and day I constantly remember you in my prayers. Recalling your tears, I long to see you, so that I may be filled with joy. I have been reminded of your sincere faith, which first lived in your grandmother Lois and in your mother Eunice and, I am persuaded, now lives in you also. For this reason I remind you to fan into flame the gift of God, which is in you through the laying on of my hands. For God did not give us a spirit of timidity, but a spirit of power, of love, and of self-discipline.*

The word "spirit" here should be capitalized, for the Holy Spirit, rather than an attitude, is meant. It is the Spirit who gives the power, love and self-discipline Timothy will need to overcome his natural "timidity" (more literally, "cowardliness or fear").

Now if you read the text thoroughly, you'll see it states, *I have been reminded of your sincere faith, which first lived in your grandmother Lois and in your mother Eunice and, I am persuaded, now lives in you also.* This tells me the same faith and spirit that lives within our parents and grandparents, lives within us as well.

My grandmother had a very strong spirit. She was deep within her belief. Regardless of how much the world tried to break her, she wouldn't allow it to interfere with her faith in her family, her belief in Christ, and more importantly, her husband. For this Christ blessed her with a very fruitful life. No one can tell me otherwise.

My grandmother lived to be ninety-two years old. She was able to tell most of her children and grandchildren good-bye before she passed. She didn't suffer from any illnesses besides arthritis, and none of her children have either. Not too many families can say that they haven't had any significant deaths in their family outside of natural causes due to old age. You cannot tell me this wasn't due to her walk of faith.

However, along the road of life, the spirit that was passed down to my mother from my grandmother became lost, and during that lost stage was when a spirit of insecurity and fear was passed down upon me. But the spirit of my grandmother's faith still lived inside us. It never died; again, it only became lost. It was buried deep within our souls, waiting for my mother, myself, or anyone within my family to reclaim and find it.

Am I saying had I not been fearful or insecure within my relationship I wouldn't have been controlling? It is a strong possibility because that fear was the root of my problem. Had I addressed the root, it's possible what had manifested within me as a child, would have been cured and the abuse ended. Even if there were more underlining issues outside of my insecurity and fear, I would have been getting help, so sooner or later they would have been discovered as well. This is why it is important to understand why I want you to look in the mirror. At any point we can stop traveling down the road we are on. We can turn around, make a right, or make a left, but we don't have to continue to go straight. Are you ready?

CHAPTER 5

WHAT IS ECONOMIC ABUSE ?

Some of you might be reading the title to this chapter and wondering what in the world I am talking about. *Economic abuse, I haven't heard of this*, you might be thinking. My reply is that because you haven't heard of it or this might not be something that is overly talked about, that doesn't mean it doesn't exist. Before we can discuss it, we first must understand exactly what it is.

Remember, an abuser's main goal is to control you, and they will frequently hurt you to do that. In addition to hurting you emotionally or possibly physically, an abusive partner may also hurt you in the pocketbook. Economic or financial abuse includes:

- Controlling the finances
- Withholding money or credit cards
- Giving you an allowance
- Making you account for every penny you spend
- Stealing from you or taking your money
- Exploiting your assets for personal gain
- Withholding basic necessities (food, clothes, medications, shelter)
- Preventing you from working or choosing your own career
- Sabotaging your job (making you miss work, calling constantly)

Though I'll be touching on each subject, for some I'll have to give you a general idea because I haven't experienced everything within my personal life. So, let's get started. It's mirror time. Keep in mind, while we are in front of the mirror, we are asking ourselves two questions: Am I allowing this to happen to me, or am I doing this to someone else?

CONTROLLING THE FINANCES

Do you feel as though everything has to go through you? Not a penny can be spent without your approval? This was me. I didn't feel as though I was controlling my partner; instead I thought I was helping her. All I was doing, though, was fooling myself into believing I was helping her. We were two separate individuals trying to live as one. That didn't mean I had the final say when it came to our money, nor did it mean she did, either. What it meant was that we needed to work together for a common ground and purpose. I needed to understand that just as with anything else in our relationship, we weren't going to always see eye to eye on how money was spent. There would be times when we disagreed as we definitely would not always make the right decisions when it came to financial matters. I learned that if we handled whatever consequences we faced due to our bad decisions together, we could get through anything. That was the key. We needed to support one another and be each other's back to lean on.

Does any of this sound familiar to you? Is this you? If so, please realize you cannot control every situation. Decisions are nothing but choices. Sometimes we make the right one and other times, we don't. However, when you are in a relationship, when you are in a marriage, you are in a union. If you work as one and as a team, you can work your way through any situation that arises. Stop controlling the finances.

WITHHOLDING MONEY OR CREDIT CARDS

In every relationship I have been in, the women have always worked. They have always had their own money and if they didn't, they had no problem spending mine. But I have seen situations where this wasn't always the case. I'll use a friend as an example.

For a long stretch, he was out of work. His wife had a very nice-paying job and she maintained the household while he was down on his luck. At first, he thought he'd only be out of work for a little bit. As the days turned into months, and employer after employer started to pass him over, the depression started to seep in for the both of them. He felt like less of a man because he wasn't pulling his weight. And she didn't know how to deal with her friends in her ear about her man. You see, friends can be the worst at times...well, associates. True friends are there to uplift, not tear down.

No woman wants a deadbeat for a man. Though this wasn't the case in their situation, that is what her friends perceived him as unemployed. The more they complained, the more they influenced her to believe them over her husband. Because of this, she tried to find ways to encourage him to get a job. What did she do? She started withholding money from him. If he wasn't bringing any home, he wasn't going to spend hers. She even went as far as canceling his credit cards and so forth.

This type of behavior in any relationship is unacceptable. All this did was made matters worse and added an extra strain on their relationship. If you are the head of the household and you have a housewife or househusband, this doesn't give you the right to dictate what the other spends or how much you are giving them. If you have the mindset that it's your money, then you do not need to be in a relationship because a partner is not what you are looking for. Do you do this? Is this you?

GIVING YOU AN ALLOWANCE

The word "allowance" says it all. I'm allowing you to spend MY money. I give my child an allowance. Usually this is for household chores that are done, good grades in school, or whatever the case may be. An allowance gives them a sense of work ethic. It shows them that if they do a good day's work, then they'll be paid for it. Your spouse or partner isn't your child. They are your partner. If you want a story for this one, read the above story for withholding money or credit cards. What I'll give you now is some advice.

Every situation is different, but I don't know too many situations where a leopard changes its spots. What I mean by that is, when you first started dating, you knew if you were dealing with a man with a great work ethic. You knew if he was going to be a provider and always have your back. Same with a woman—you knew if she was strong-willed, always needed to be employed and pushed for excellence at work. I'm sure this is part of what attracted you to them while dating.

You also knew if your man was lazy or if your woman had no drive or work ethic. However, something else attracted you to them. You fell in love with them for other reasons. Stop concentrating on the negative and concentrate on why you fell in love with them. Don't use putting them on an allowance as a punishing method or teaching tool. There is nothing wrong with change, but it can't be forced. It has to be accepted. Don't think that if you deprive them of money or keep them on an allowance, this will bring about change because it will not. It will only cause resentment and further damage your relationship.

MAKING YOU ACCOUNT FOR EVERY PENNY YOU SPEND

This is an easy one. There is no denying whether or not you are doing this or if this is being done to you. Now I laugh at it, but it's only because I've spent hours and hours in therapy getting help with my controlling behavior. At the time it was no laughing matter. I remember once the woman I was with every day would take the receipts out of her pocket and put them on the dresser to show me where her money was spent. I didn't ask for this, but I asked so much what she was doing with her money, she had everything ready for me to review on a daily basis.

It's no wonder the relationship didn't work. Who wants to live like that? At the time, I thought nothing of it. I actually thought she was being a smart ass by saving the receipts and leaving them on the dresser for me to review, but then it became easier for me to track so I didn't complain or care. In my mind, I thought I was helping her budget her money, but all I was doing was trying to control how she was spending her money. The minute I saw a receipt for a personal item she'd bought herself that I deemed wasn't necessary, an argument erupted. The key is that *I* deemed unnecessary. I needed someone to set me aside and ask me, "Who are you?"

Here it was, she was putting in forty-hour work weeks, but yet she couldn't even spend her money on something for herself without her man having something to say about it. Home is supposed to be your sanctuary. It's supposed to be your peace of mind from the stresses of the world. Due to my controlling ways, she didn't have that at home. Don't strip your spouse or partner of having peace. Don't make the same mistake I made. If this is you, let it go. If your partner has problems budgeting money spent for personal items over bills, work together to devise a solution. But don't become a tax auditor and audit every dime he or she spends.

STEALING FROM YOU OR TAKING YOUR MONEY

No one likes a thief. They can't be trusted and you definitely don't want to lie beside one every night. Now if you have the type of relationship where if you leave money on the dresser and it's cool if your spouse or partner takes it, then that is fine. I don't consider that stealing and more importantly, neither do you. That is the agreement between the two of you. Now if this is happening and you don't approve it, then that is a different story. I hope you would have said something about it by now, so I'll keep it moving.

Let's say you go in your partner's pockets to see how much money he left in his pants so you can pocket it. Or that you wait until your wife gets in the shower to go through her purse and take her loose dollars, thinking she won't miss them or didn't account for them. If this is true, then there is a problem. This also goes for if you have access to the other's bank account and deduct money without permission. Though I rarely put the blame on the person this is happening to, in this situation I will.

If you allow your partner to steal from you with no consequences, such as telling them it's not acceptable or leaving the relationship if they continue to steal from you, then you are enabling them. Your actions are telling them, this is acceptable and they will continue to steal from you. So this time I'll ask, are you allowing this? If so, you need to raise your bar of standards. You need to tell your spouse or partner this is not acceptable and if they ignore it, you need to end the relationship. A person can and will only do what you allow. Raise your bar, tell them this is not acceptable and make sure they comply with your standard.

EXPLOITING YOUR ASSETS FOR PERSONAL GAIN

This one might be a hard one to discuss. My biggest asset is my mind. Financial assets, though, I can't say I have those on the resume. Being serious, this again goes to the character of the person you have chosen to be with. My only advice in this situation would be to take the time to get to know the person prior to committing to them. Things are so rushed these days. No one really wants to date and take the time to get to know a person. They presume the representative they've met for the first couple of months is the actual person. Now four months have passed and you are moving in with him or her.

You don't know this person or their motives. You know their representative. You really want to get to know the person and that takes time. Try years, not months. After a while, the representative will not be able to continue to stay on display. The true person and their true intentions will eventually rise to the surface. If you come from money or make good money, there is nothing wrong with a prenuptial agreement. Most say, "No, I'm not signing a prenuptial agreement." Then my response would be, "Cool, then we don't need to get married."

A prenuptial agreement is nothing but a sound *business* decision. This protects you and your assets from someone who is only interested in personal gain. Remember you are supposed to be marrying a person for love. If your marriage is God ordained, why are you thinking about divorce? Divorce shouldn't even be in your mindset. That is the only reason why you are opposed to have a prenuptial agreement. Because you know if the marriage doesn't work out and a prenuptial agreement is in play, you get nothing. Now you might think I'm contradicting myself and you possibly could be right. But I don't know too many marriages that didn't work because of a prenuptial agreement. As a matter of fact, I don't know any. If the marriage ended the day you signed it, it never started. The marriage ended because of something else. I got my money by being a smart businessman. So the smart business decision is to protect your assets. For those who disagree, let's agree to disagree.

WITHHOLDING BASIC NECESSITIES (FOOD, CLOTHING, MEDICATION, SHELTER)

This one is very troubling because we are talking about adults. If you do this to your spouse, I am not judging you. If you are allowing this to happen to you, I am not looking down upon you. I only want to bring change. Remember we are talking about two individuals in a relationship. Two people who love each other. This isn't how you show love. You do not withhold necessities from your partner because they are not doing what you want them to do.

I don't know too many situations where clothes, food, medication, or shelter are withheld from a person, so I won't touch on that aspect. I'll give you another situation. Now, let me clarify. I'm not saying that this doesn't happen. I'm only saying that I, personally, do not know too many situations. I will touch on sex. That is a basic necessity, whether you want to admit it or not. I know...we are talking about economic or financial abuse. Sex isn't either, but sex is used as a form of punishment because of it.

The abuser withholds the basic necessities, attempting to control their partner financially. Sex is another form of punishment. Ladies, stop laughing. Withholding on the loving to a brother is cruel punishment. It's a form of control. Fellas, this goes for you, too! Though you might not be laughing, you often don't want to give your woman any because you are in your feelings. She didn't do what you wanted. She went out and spent three hundred dollars on a pair of shoes and you can't understand why. It's not for you to understand. As long as home is taken care of, that is all that should matter.

PREVENTING YOU FROM WORKING OR CHOOSING YOUR OWN CAREER

I touched on this briefly in the story "I'm Going Out Tonight." Lena had just had the baby and I really didn't want her working. I thought of every excuse under the sun for her not to. Once the excuses didn't work, I was going to try to find other ways to control the situation and keep her out of work. You ask me now why, I can't tell you. In the beginning, I thought financially it would make more sense to be at home with our child. We wouldn't have to pay for day care and that would be one less cost.

Granted, we would've had more money coming into the house if she had been working, but I didn't see it that way. Now older and wiser, I think part of me felt if she had found a career, I'd have lost a part of her. She wouldn't be as reliant on me. Every man wants to feel like he is needed. I think it's a part of our inner being. We want our women to rely on us or feel that sense of being the backbone; the one they can lean on. My mother was an independent career woman. She relied on no one. If she wanted it, she worked for it.

Though I want my daughter to have that same characteristic trait, I didn't want my spouse or partner to. Backward, huh? I know! I try not to gender bash, but this goes out to the men. Stop preventing your wife or girlfriend from working. You are not their father. You are their partner. If they ask your opinion on what you think about their options, give good advice. Give your honest opinion and help them make the best decision. The key word is "help." Do not hinder. That is the sign of a real man. A real man uplifts his woman. He doesn't hinder her. He wants her to be all she can be and more.

SABOTAGING YOUR JOB (MAKING YOU MISS WORK, CALLING CONSTANTLY)

I have a friend whose wife calls him constantly while he is at work. She knows he has a job to do, but she'll call repeatedly through-out the day to continue an argument from the night prior, or simply to irritate him. I could never figure why. I mean, she would call back to back to back. She would even rotate phones to call. She'd go from calling his desk phone to his cell phone, if he didn't answer. One day he had eighty-four missed calls. He didn't know what to do. He knew he had reached his wit's end; however, he loved this woman dearly. All he wanted to do was work through whatever problem they were having.

Then it hit me. She knew this was the only way she could get through to him. She figured, since she was at work miserable, why not ruin his day as well. She was spiteful. All this did was make matters worse. What if he had the type of position where his supervisor was always around? The likeliest result would have been he would have lost his job. Then what would she have done? Her actions would have been the cause of it. You can't tell me that would have made matters better at home.

No, his natural reaction would have been to be pissed. He definitely would have resented her. Notwithstanding, their house-hold still had to be considered. She couldn't have maintained the monthly bills alone on her income. She would have needed his income, but none of that mattered to her at the time. However, it would have smacked her right in the face had he been fired. If this is you, remember for every action there is a reaction.

Wow, WE TOUCHED ON A LOT WITHIN THIS CHAPTER. It is only about to get deeper from here. I wasn't fortunate enough to catch my issues within the exposure or manifestation stages. It took me transforming into what I hated for me to rush for help. In some situations, that is what it takes, but it doesn't have to for you. I often ask each of you to look into the mirror and ask yourself if this is you.

Have you recently been exposed to abuse by your parents or your former boyfriend or girlfriend? Have you started to see signs of what you witnessed in your past manifesting within you? If so, please get help. Therapy isn't a crutch but a means of dealing with the issues that we are faced with. Talking to someone always helps. If you don't want to seek out a therapist, try a counselor, pastor or priest.

I'd stay away from friends and family. They tend to not give objective advice—especially if they are going through a similar situation or don't know the true definition of a real relationship. Remember, communication is the key to all. It's not too late to sit down and talk to your partner while in the exposure or manifestation stage. Once you allow it to transform you into what you fear most, it's only going to bring more pain to both you and the one you love.

3rd Stage
TRANSFORMATION (ENTRANCE)

TO CHANGE IN CHARACTER OR CONDITION

Entrance

1. Power or permission to enter
2. The act of entering
3. The means or place of entry

ROUND ONE

Lena sat in the house, fuming. Our relationship was an exact mirror of my mother and Stanley's, whether I wanted to admit it or not. The only difference was I played the roles of both my mother and Stanley from time to time. It depended on the situation. I never put my hands on Lena, but then again, I never had to either. Usually Lena would get so upset her actions would be funny and very easy to ignore.

I knew she'd be pissed when I walked into the door. I'd been gone all day and, to make matters worse, I had lied to her earlier about where I was going and who I was going to be with. There was a young lady, Janae, who was temping at the job and whom I'd grown quite fond of. It wasn't anything sexual. We simply had very good chemistry and could really talk. With all that was going on at home, I needed some sort of outlet, and she provided that by just listening. Since she was new in town, I promised to show her around.

In order to do this, I lied and told Lena I had a basketball tournament and that she couldn't go because it might take all day, depending on the more our team won. I knew Lena like the back of my hand and knew that she wouldn't want to sit around a gym all day, so that was the perfect cover-up. I didn't anticipate Lena's wisdom of me, though. The touring trip with Janae wasn't something that was planned. She'd asked at the last minute and I agreed. I didn't have time to prepare Lena for my lie. I'd played in many tournaments, some that lasted all day, so that part was believable. But I always told Lena well in advance about them. This time I didn't. I told her as I was getting dressed to leave in the morning to meet my friend.

I wanted to cut my time with Janae short, but we were having so much fun, it made that hard and inconceivable. I hadn't had fun with Lena in a long time. Janae knew I was in a serious relationship and she wasn't the type of woman to try to come between that. At least, that is what I thought. They say a woman knows another woman's actions better than a man does. I believe it. However, I wasn't interested in sleeping with anyone other than Lena. I only wanted to have a little fun and Janae was simply that.

I walked into a dimly lit house. There were hardly any lights on. My instincts told me to crash on the couch. I could feel an argument brewing. Against my better judgment, I walked into the bedroom, hoping Lena was asleep. As I should have known, she wasn't. She was sitting up watching TV as if she were waiting for me to come home. The baby was sleeping in the crib.

"How was the game?" she asked.

If I was skeptical at first, I wasn't anymore. Something was wrong. It didn't matter when I'd come in the house, Lena always greeted me with a kiss and asked about my day. The only time she didn't was when she was pissed. I started to panic because I realized she knew something. But what? Her intention was to set me up for a steep fall. However, I wasn't going to fall for it.

"I need to tell you something," I replied.

"What's up?"

"I lied about the tournament. I didn't have one today. Instead there was a temp at work, Janae, who I'm cool with, and she's new to the area. I showed her around and stuff and we kicked it today. It wasn't anything serious, though; just as friends."

"Friends, huh? So let me get this straight. You lied to me by telling me that you had a tournament today, but the whole time you were out on a date with some chick you work with. And you want me to believe it is nothing serious?"

"Yes, it wasn't a date. I swear! We just hung out. I showed her a couple of hangout spots and so forth. It wasn't anything serious."

Amused by my response, Lena started to laugh.

"You left here at a little after seven a.m. and it's almost midnight. What did you do? Show her the entire metropolitan area? You know what; that doesn't even matter. So where did you pick her up from, since you showed her around? That means you drove, right?"

"Yes, I drove. I picked her up from her hotel. What does that have to do with anything?"

"Oh, it has a lot to do with it. So that means you dropped her back off at her hotel also, huh? How long did you stay there?"

"What makes you think I went in? I could have just dropped her off and left."

"Don't talk to me like I'm stupid. Now you want to be honest, then be honest. If you want to finish lying like you started out the day, then do that. But please don't talk to me like I'm stupid."

"Yes, I went to her hotel room. We finished dinner at around eight or so and she was getting tired. We did a lot of walking today. So we went up and talked a little more and watched a movie. After that, I left."

"What the hell? You watched a movie!"

"Baby…"

Lena cut me off.

"Damn, I thought dinner and a movie was a date. I mean, I can't even get that, but some random chick who you barely know does. Wow! So you watch a movie, do a little talking and that's it, you just leave?"

"Yes, I swear. We didn't have sex, or anything like that. We didn't kiss or hug, I mean, nothing. I promise you. I wouldn't cheat on you. I wouldn't disrespect our relationship."

"You wouldn't what? You spent the day with another damn woman while I was stuck up in the house and you don't feel like that was disrespecting our relationship. You don't feel like you were cheating. I'd rather you'd got some. I mean, at least it would have been worth it then."

"Huh, why would you wish I had sex with another woman? Baby, I didn't cheat on you. It's no secret we have been having problems. We spent the majority of the day talking about my problems, and she was telling me about the problems she is having with her husband. She is married. I keep telling you; it wasn't like that. We are only friends."

Lena got up out of the bed and started to put her clothes on.

"Where are you going?" I asked.

Lena continued to ignore me and kept getting dressed. Once she had her clothes on, she went over to the dresser and started to take her clothes out of it and packed a bag.

"So, I tell you the truth and you are going to leave me? I didn't do anything with her. You think I cheated on you and I didn't."

"What the hell do you think you did? You went and confided in another woman. You went and gave her a part of yourself that belongs to me. If we are having problems, we need to discuss them. Not you running off to some chick you randomly know and telling her our business. Then you were in her hotel room. We haven't had sex in close to a month. I know you did something. You must think I'm a fool. You must really think I'm dumb. First, you feed me this bullshit story about you having a tournament today and then I find out you spent the entire day with another woman. You were with her for over sixteen hours, Harell. I can't get two hours of your time but this woman is so special she gets sixteen hours of your time. Well, you know what, she can have you."

"I don't want her. Look, come on; let's just talk about this," I pleaded.

I realized my actions were wrong but I honestly didn't plan on Lena finding out what I'd done earlier today. Every relationship has secrets. I was hoping this would remain one. I was at a loss for words and really didn't know how to fix the situation, which only frustrated me more. To top it off, she was acting as if she didn't care anymore, and I was losing my mind.

"Now you want to talk about it. What is that? The advice she gave you? She told you to come home and talk to me about our problems, or is this your way of trying to fix the situation? Yeah, that's it. Well, you are about…hmmm…sixteen hours too late to talk. That is something you should have wanted to do this morning before you snuck out of here to be with another woman."

"First of all, I didn't sneak out!"

"I call leaving before I get up sneaking off but, then again, it's obvious we don't think alike because I wouldn't have gone talking to another man about our problems in our relationship. And I damn sure wouldn't have sat up and lied to you like you were nothing. I have a little more respect for you and our relationship than that. But hey, again, we don't think alike."

"Why does everything have to be a smart comment? That is why I can't talk to you. You always want to be smart about every damn thing. Can you ever take anything seriously?"

"Oh, please believe, I take this very seriously. You are going to see just how seriously I do take it when you wake up by yourself because I'm done. You can have her or she can have you. Regardless, I'm done!"

"So, you are just going to leave me? That is it. After all these years, you are going to up and leave? Fine; leave then. You never gave a shit about me anyway. You were always quick to run. It's cool; I don't even care. It hurts, but I don't care. Leave then, Lena."

"Don't try to turn this around on me. This is your doing. You went and confided in another woman. You are the one who stepped out on me. You damn right, I'm leaving. I'm tired. I know we have problems, but you make it seem like you have the answer. If so, why haven't I heard it? You can run out and talk to John and anyone else, but you never talk to me. I'm the one who you need to be talking to, and then this. You go run to some stranger."

Finally, Lena started to get emotional. Finally, I got a sense of what my actions had done to her. She was obviously hurt. I went over to try to console her.

"Get away from me. Please, do not touch me. Go and touch her. Go and console her about her husband and her problems. At least she has a husband. I can't even get a ring, but hey, I guess I don't deserve one."

Her words cut through me like no knife ever could. I started to really think my actions had cost me her. I grabbed a hold of her.

"Get off of me, Harell. I'm leaving. I'm tired of this. I'm sick of you mistreating me. I love you. I will always love you, but we do not need to be together."

"Baby, please! I'm sorry. I just felt like I needed to get away. I was wrong for that. You're right! I should have come to you to talk."

Lena continued to try to pry my hands off of her, to loosen my grasp. I wouldn't let go, though. If I did, the chances of her walking out of that door were very high. And who knew whether or not she was going to return.

"Harell, get off of me!" Lena yelled.

I continued to ignore her. She then tried to bend my fingers back. I tried as long as possible to ignore the pain. I didn't want to let go, but it really started to hurt. Finally, I released my grasp.

"I told you, do not put your hands on me," Lena said as she swung. Her punch glanced off my shoulder. I quickly reacted and grabbed her by her throat and slammed her into the wall.

"Have you lost your damn mind? Have you? I told you about putting your hands on me. Don't you ever put your hands on me! I will kill you up in here. You keep playing me like I'm some sucka or something. You talk to everyone else like that, not me. Do you hear me?"

My grasp around Lena's neck was very tight. She could barely breathe, let alone talk. Scared, she simply nodded her head. Tears were welling up in her eyes. I quickly released my grasp around her neck and stopped choking her. I walked out of the room, trying to calm myself down. Lena fell to the floor and started crying. This wasn't the first time she had put her hands on me. She did it often but never had I retaliated. I always was the bigger person and tried to defuse the situation. This time, however, was different. I reacted instead.

I sat down on the couch in the living room, waiting for Lena to exit the room. Instead she locked the bedroom door so I couldn't get back in. I kept telling myself over and over again, she had no right to put her hands on me. I wasn't trying to hurt her. I just didn't want her to leave. I was only hugging her. She had no right! All of this could have been avoided. This wasn't my fault! It couldn't have been my fault. I didn't have a choice. I had to do what I did or she would've continued to think I was soft, and she could put her hands on me. I did what a man would do, didn't I?

CHAPTER 2

ROUND TWO

I was in severe pain. I'd recently had surgery to repair a torn patella tendon in my left knee. I had suffered it earlier in the basketball season, playing for the company team. In the beginning Lena was very supportive. She took off the first week after my surgery to take care of me. She waited on me hand and foot. I was so appreciative. After all that we had been through, I actually was shocked. It showed how much she really loved me. Our relationship was always on again, off again. After a while, I just became accustomed to it. However, I didn't expect her to go all out as she had.

One week, though, quickly changed into four. My leg was still immobilized. The doctor anticipated I'd be able to start therapy to build the strength back up in my leg in six weeks. I only had two more to go. I didn't know who would be more pleased, me or Lena. I wasn't the easiest patient to handle. At times, I could be a very big baby. Factor in this was my first serious injury and I was pretty much unbearable to live with.

Lena decided to get a drink after work. She needed one to prepare to work her second job, which was taking care of me. Plus, she needed some time alone. She didn't have to worry about picking the kids up from day care. I was home hurt, so the kids stayed home with me. Lena didn't plan on being out long. Maybe an hour or two tops, but one drink quickly turned into several, and two hours was now going on five.

I hadn't heard from her since earlier in the day and she hadn't mentioned her intentions to get a drink. She knew I would have been opposed to it and would have wanted her to come home. Plus, an hour or two late wouldn't have made a difference. I possibly wouldn't have noticed.

I tried repeatedly to reach her on her cell phone, however, it kept going straight to voicemail. It started to become obvious to me that I couldn't wait for her to come home and make the kids dinner any longer. It was late and they needed to eat. I grabbed my crutches and got out of the bed. It was still hard to maneuver around. I had to keep my left leg totally straight and still couldn't put any real pressure on it yet.

At my last doctor's appointment, I'd had another X-ray and MRI to make sure the tendon and my bone structure was healing properly. Though the tendon was correctly mending, it still wasn't strong. Too much activity could cause it to rupture again and I'd have to start the process all over again. I was ordered by the doctors to be on my feet as little as possible.

However, I had no choice. If I didn't feed my kids, no one would. It wasn't like I had anyone I could call at the time to come over and help. By the time anyone would have arrived, more than likely the kids would have been asleep, and it would have defeated the purpose of calling. This was totally unlike Lena. She and I battled a lot but she made sure our problems never became the kids' problem. She knew how to differentiate the two. Something had to have happened to her. This was totally unlike her. No phone call, nothing. Something surely had to have been wrong. That was the only explanation I could think of.

I juggled back and forth between fixing something small and quick for the kids to eat and calling any and everyone to see if they had heard anything from Lena. First stop had to be Maxine.

Though I hated her, I knew if Lena made plans, she would call Maxine to fill her in on the details. I didn't expect Maxine to tell me much. She would never betray her girl's trust. But I knew that regardless of what she told me, she would be able to get in touch with Lena and let her know I was looking for her. At this point, all I wanted to know was that Lena was alright. The minute Lena heard from Maxine, it wouldn't have been long before Lena was calling me with some type of excuse. I would have known I had another problem on my hands, but at least I would have known she was fine and not hurt or anything.

Maxine sounded surprised that Lena wasn't home. If she was acting, she definitely was in the wrong profession. I didn't get the sense that she was lying. If Lena was up to something, Maxine would have been the first to know. This made matters worse. Now I was starting to panic. It wasn't another guy. It had to be something serious. This is the first time I wished she was cheating.

Though Lena and her mother weren't close, she still tried to help her mother as much as possible for her little brothers. She was very close to them. Maybe she had to go over there and she lost track of time talking with them. That definitely was a possibility. At that point, it was all that I could think of. The small bit of hope I had quickly faded. Lena's mother hadn't heard from her, either.

My mind started to race. Every time I thought of a situation that could have happened, it was quickly proven wrong and dismissed. It was hard to think this situation was going to have a positive outcome. It had only been five hours, so the police couldn't do anything. She had to be missing for over twenty-four hours before I could file a missing person's report, and calling around to emergency rooms was nothing but another dead-end street. They wouldn't even tell me if they had a patient with her name. To top it off, Tre was irritable and cranky because it was getting late and he still hadn't eaten.

My nerves were at full tilt. I tried my best not to take it out on the kids, but I was on one leg, in pain, and had no clue where Lena was. I made sure the kids ate quickly and went to bed. The sooner I got them out of the way, at least that would be one thing off the list. Part of me thought I would maybe be able to relax a little, with that part done. I was wrong. I sat on the couch, praying everything was alright. I'd seen this situation on TV time and time again. Innocent people no longer needed reasons to be abducted or killed.

I tried Lena's cell phone again; however, it continued to go to voicemail. If I couldn't reach her, neither could anyone else, but I decided to call Maxine again. The minute I got off the phone with her earlier, she would have called Lena to find out what was going on. I hoped Maxine had more luck reaching her than I had. Of course, luck wasn't on my side tonight. Maxine said she left her a message on her voicemail and Lena still hadn't called her back yet. She did pretty much the same as the rest of us did. That was all we could do.

As I hung up the phone, my emotions started to get the best of me. Though it was late, I decided to call my grandmother. She was the only person who could calm me down. She never saw the glass as half empty but, instead, she saw it as half full. She tried her best to calm me down, but this was the only time it wasn't working. I couldn't even stay concentrated on her. While she was talking, all I could think about was Lena. My grandmother was a woman of God, so before she would let me off the phone, we prayed together. After I got off the phone with my grandmother, emotionally I was drained. I lay on the couch. I was helpless. There was nothing I could do.

As time passed, I eventually fell asleep waiting. The sound of Lena's key in the door woke me. It was close to 2 a.m. She stumbled into the house, singing. I was furious. I got up from the couch without my crutch. The pain in my knee wasn't even a factor.

"Where the hell have you been?" I asked once she closed the front door.

"Hey there, baby!" she slurred. She was smiling like nothing was wrong. It was evident she was drunk, but I wondered why.

"Where the hell have you been?" I asked again.

"I heard you the first time. You don't have to keep asking me the same damn question over and over again."

I tried to remain calm. I didn't want the situation to escalate further than needed.

"Okay, I'm going to let that slide since you have been drinking."

"You don't have to let nothing slide. I don't know who you think you are. You must think someone is scared of you or something. Where have I been? I don't have to answer to you. I've been out. Duh! I wasn't with you."

"What is wrong with you?"

"Nothing is wrong with me. What is wrong with you?" she replied.

"Something obviously is wrong with you. Do you realize how worried I was? I didn't know what happened to you. Who goes out drinking and doesn't have the common courtesy to call anyone to let them know they're okay? I've called everyone. I've called your mom. I called Maxine. I have been worried sick. I was even calling hospitals. I didn't know what had happened to you."

"Did I ask you to call anyone? What are you calling my mother and Max for? I don't want everyone in my business. I'm grown. If I wanted you to know where I was, then obviously I would have called you and told you. I don't need to check in."

"Look! First of all, you know I can only do but so much. I just had surgery on my knee. I'm not even supposed to be up on it. I'm on bedrest. You know this."

"It's always something with you. You can't do this or you can't do that. It's always something! I'm not your mother. You are not my child. You aren't my responsibility."

"But these kids are! They are your responsibility and how were they supposed to eat if you weren't here? Even if you didn't want to take care of me, that's fine. I'm grown, but the kids have nothing to do with this. You left them out high and dry."

"The last time I checked, you were their father. They are your responsibility as well. I can be sick, weak, or tired, but I still do what is necessary for them. Why can't you? What makes you so different? Why do you have a different set of rules?"

"I'm not different. I don't have a different set of nothing. You see I fed them tonight. That wasn't even my point. My point was…"

"It doesn't even matter what your point is. You fed them, good job, but look who is standing over there bitching about it. That is your responsibility as a parent and you're sitting here complaining. For real, you are blowing my high right now. I had a good time tonight. I had some *me* time. I think I'm going to start doing that at least once a week. Yeah, I think so. Anyway, move, I don't have anything else to say to you."

I quickly grabbed Lena by her throat and choked her up against the wall.

"You aren't going to stand in front of me and disrespect me like I'm nothing. Have you lost your damn mind? I don't know who has you feeling like you are America's Next Top Model or something but you aren't. Keep talking to me like you've lost your mind here. Keep playing with me."

The look in Lena's eyes should have said it all. She didn't show one ounce of fear. It was as if she wanted me to react. She had a look of anger in her eyes. Without hesitation, she kicked me in my surgically repaired knee. The pain rushed through my body. I quickly released my grasp of her and dropped to the floor. Lena kicked me in my side.

"Don't you ever put your damn hands on me again! I've told you before, I'm not your child. This is the last time you touch me."

Lena kicked me again and then went into the kitchen. I heard her rumbling around in the kitchen drawer. There was nothing in there for her to be looking for but trouble. I got up off the floor and limped into the kitchen. Once I was in there, I saw Lena had a knife in her hand. I quickly sidestepped her as she rushed me and I grabbed her arm with the knife. Lena was furious. She was trying to stab me. I twisted her arm. Lena let out a scream as she dropped the knife. I clearly could overpower her. I grabbed the back of her neck and pushed her face up into the cabinet.

"What the hell is wrong with you? You want to kill me? Huh, is that what you want? Have you lost your damn mind?"

Lena was flinging her arms and legs, trying desperately to hit me somehow. I was very protective of my knee, so the closer she got, the more I'd move. Finally, I released her. I braced myself for a battle. Shockingly, she was calm.

"You are weak. That is all you are. You can beat on me, but please believe if I was a man, you wouldn't. All you are is a punk," Lena said.

Her words cut like a dagger. Beat on her? Outside of when I had been caught with Janae, I had never put my hands on her. I'd seen my mother get beaten. She didn't know what being beat meant. I had no respect for her. I spat in Lena's face.

"I'm through! Get your stuff and get the hell out of my house!" I said.

I turned to walk out of the kitchen. I wasn't going to continue to live like this. She'd gone out and didn't even have the common courtesy to call. Then she wasn't even woman enough to apologize for her actions. I couldn't do this anymore. Before I knew it, I felt a sharp pain at the back of my head. Lena had picked up the baby's high chair and hit me with it. I quickly went down. That didn't matter to her. She hit me again in my leg for good measure. Thankfully, she missed my knee. However, I was in severe pain. Lena went into the bedroom and grabbed a few of my clothes and threw them in a bag. She tossed it on the floor in front of me where I was lying.

"This is my house. If anyone is leaving, it will be you. Good night!" she said, and then went into the bedroom. She didn't even lock the door. All I could do was lie on the floor and cry. My knee was killing me. I took my immobilizing brace off to look at my knee. It was bleeding. Three of my stitches had popped and pus was also coming from my knee. Even with all that, what hurt most was how little Lena viewed me as a man.

CHAPTER 3

THE FINAL ROUND

Something was wrong. My intuition was running high. Usually intuition and men don't go hand in hand—probably because we may have it, but we never listen or pay any attention to it. We choose to ignore what is right in front of our face or make excuses for what it is we see. I wasn't that way, though. The minute my antennas went up to something being wrong, I wanted to know what was what. That was the only way I would be able to map out my game plan on how I would handle whatever the situation was.

It was obvious Lena was seeing someone else. Her actions said as much, but I still had no actual physical proof to accuse her. One night earlier in the week, I was tired from a long day at work, so I decided to get in the bed a little earlier than usual. Lena was lying in the bed talking on her cell phone. The minute she realized I was getting in the bed, she left out of the room and closed the door behind her as if she had something to hide. That was a first. Usually, she would continue with whatever conversation she was having. My presence in the room wouldn't have mattered... At that point, I started to pay attention to her actions more closely.

I noticed a change in her demeanor. Usually we talked throughout the day, either by text or phone call. All of that had stopped. We barely interacted anymore. I had been so long that I couldn't remember the last time she had called or texted me. If I wasn't getting her time, someone else was.

Being a man, a part of me didn't want to face that reality. I wanted to believe I was overreacting. I could have easily proven my theory right or wrong, but I was also scared to be right. By us being on the same cell phone account, I had access to all of her incoming and outgoing calls, even her sent or received text messages. However, I didn't check the records. Instead, I threw out hints to Lena that I would or already had checked them. I hoped she would come clean and tell me what was going on, but she ignored me. She continued to say she wasn't doing anything. She wasn't cheating.

Once that Friday finally came around, I needed the weekend more than the next man. I needed some time to myself to clear my thoughts. I knew Lena wouldn't be at home. She had gone out both Friday and Saturday for the past three weeks. We barely spent any time together anymore. Even when we were blessed to have a baby sitter, I still saw no part of her. She was back to her old tricks and hitting the streets. I didn't even bother to ask with whom. It didn't matter. The more I said, the more she tuned me out. It was useless. I had run out of ways and the energy to fight for us any more.

I knew what direction our relationship was heading and though I didn't want it to go there, there was nothing I could do to stop it. She had to want things to work as much as I did; it was obvious she didn't. The only reason she stayed as long as she did was for the children. It had stopped being about her love for me a long time ago.

I got into the house and started to get the kids ready. They were spending the weekend away. Once their rides came to pick each of them up, I went into my room and lay down for a bit. I wanted to relax before I went to John's house, or wherever the wind took me. Lena came in the house and didn't say one word. She went into the kitchen and quickly fixed her a sandwich as if she hadn't had lunch earlier. She came into the bedroom and started to lay out her clothes for the night.

A part of me wanted to say something then, but I couldn't bring myself to find the right words. I'd seen this type of behavior before and always said it wouldn't be my relationship. This is exactly how Stanley and my mother had acted toward each other. In the beginning, Lena and I were inseparable. On weekends, with or without the kids, you'd catch us curled up together on the couch, cuddling and watching movies. I didn't need the outside world, because I had her.

However, it didn't become long before I wasn't enough for her. I couldn't even blame it all on her. I recognized that I played my role in our disconnection. I just didn't know how to fix it. Once I'd lost her interest, she had to find a way to reclaim it. Plus, part of me always felt like she thought by being in a committed relationship, she was missing out on something. I didn't know whether she was living vicariously through Maxine or any of her other friends who could go from club to club and meet guy after guy and have no one to answer to. I wasn't even sure if it was due to problems from her childhood that she had suppressed deep inside her.

But what I did know was that I no longer completed her. She needed to be out and about. If she had suppressed whatever feelings she had inside her when we first got together, trying to make us work and build a serious relationship, we didn't have the correct foundation. When you suppress something, sooner or later it will resurface because it is still within your system. It hasn't been expunged. It is still a part of your inner being.

I got out of the bed and put my shoes on. It wouldn't be long before I said something to her. At that time, I was too angry and hurt inside. These two weren't a good combination when you wanted to have a peaceful conversation. I grabbed my keys by the door and noticed she had left her cell phone there. That only made matters worse. It was obvious she was trying to hide something from me in her cell phone.

Before I knew it, I had grabbed her phone and headed out the front door. I went through everything in her phone. I went through the phone book; the inbox; I even checked her voicemail. Each time one name was apparent: Mike. He had left her a voicemail message earlier in the day, asking her to call him. There was a draft for an incomplete text message that she was going to send Mike. It was blank, however. She had deleted her inbox and sent box, so there was nothing there for me to see. Then there was the entry of Mike's phone number into her address book.

I needed a computer and fast. I went to my cousin's house that was down the street. A part of me prayed she was home. She would know exactly how to calm me down and deal with the situation the correct way. However, with my luck, she wasn't home. Her daughter let me in and I got on the computer instead. I pulled up the phone records and saw that she had spent the bulk of the past seven days talking to Mike. The records showed conversations between the two of them that lasted for hours at a time, even conversations with him while I was home but in the living room. My suspicion about Tuesday night when she'd left the room was correct. She was on the phone with him.

I felt so hurt. It is one thing if your woman gives her body to another man, that is a different kind of pain, but she was giving him something more precious—her heart. She was replacing him with me in the space that only I should have dwelled in. I tried with every ounce of my body not to cry. I wasn't going to cry there. Not in front of my little cousin. I wished her mother was home so badly. I really needed someone to talk to. I couldn't believe this was happening to me.

I needed answers and there was no way I could get them while there. There was only one person who could give me the answers that I searched for. I left and got back in my car and headed home. Coincidentally, her phone rang while I was in the car; it was Mike. I answered the phone.

"Hello."

"Can I speak to Lena?"

"Naw, you can't. Who the hell are you and why are you calling my fiancée?"

"What, Slim, you need to ask Lena who I am to her. Don't be questioning me."

"Excuse you? I'm asking you, who the hell are you and why are you calling my woman?"

He hung up the phone. I was furious. He sounded so confident and cocky at the same time, telling me that I needed to ask her who he was to her. What! My blood was boiling. If I could have had five minutes alone with Mike, I would have shown him exactly who he was to her. He wasn't anything. It was evident he knew who I was though, but didn't care. Why he didn't care, that I didn't know, but I was pretty sure it had something to do with whatever Lena had been telling him. I wasn't sure if she was telling him she was planning on leaving me or whatever the case may have been. I couldn't get home fast enough.

I walked into the house and saw Lena in the kitchen. She was furious.

"Where is my phone?" she asked.

"I don't know where your phone is, but we need to talk."

"About what? I don't have anything to say to you. You always want to talk when you're ready but never when I come to you."

"Lena, I want to ask you one question. When are you moving out?" I asked.

"June 1st," she quickly shot back at me. It was close to the end of April. June 1st was only a month away. I wasn't expecting her to respond like that. It was apparent she had already been thinking about leaving me and had mapped out her plan. All I could think about was this was so she could be with Mike.

"When were you going to tell me this? I mean, how long have you known you were leaving? You didn't feel I needed to know that. I mean, here it is I'm thinking…" I calmed myself down. It didn't take a genius to see that I was hurt. I needed to regain composure over my emotions. If I didn't, she would have been in total control of the situation because I was out of control.

"Do you love him?"

"Huh, what are you talking about?"

"I know you are cheating, so please don't lie to me."

"I'm not going to lie. I'm tired of lying and hiding things. I don't have to hide anything. I'm not cheating on you because I'm not in a relationship with you. The relationship has been over for a long time now. All we do is live together, but this definitely isn't a relationship. We don't even communicate."

"I can't believe you are going to sit there and say this. After all the shit I have put up with from you, you are going to just sit there and…"

"I just want to go; please move, so I can leave. It doesn't even matter anymore. I don't want to fight or argue with you. I just want to leave."

Before I knew it, I had swung on Lena. The punch was wild and completely missed her. I'd never swung on Lena, or any woman for that matter. Fear filled Lena as she didn't know what to do.

"You need to back up and calm down, Harell, please. I'm just trying to leave. Just back up and calm down," she said.

I grabbed her by her neck and slammed her head hard onto the kitchen cabinets repeatedly.

"You want to leave me for some other nigga! I will kill your ass! I will kill you! I swear I will!" I yelled.

Lena screamed for help. She didn't care who heard her as long as someone heard her. She screamed for someone to call 9-1-1, but no one did. I released my grasp of her neck and looked at her.

"Please, just let me leave. Please!" she cried.

I couldn't believe she still wanted to go and be with him. That was her main concern—to go and be with a man whom she barely knew, who hadn't been with her through thick and thin. I swung again. This time the punch landed and hit her on the right side of her face by her eye. She fell back and started to cry. I saw she was wounded and stopped. I was too upset to console her. She wanted to leave me, so I was going to make sure she got exactly what she wanted tonight and not another minute later. I went into the bedroom and started to grab anything she had in the closet.

The minute I left out the kitchen, Lena sprinted for the front door. She went to the neighbors and borrowed their phone to call the police and her family. I didn't care. I wanted her out of my house. I wasn't going to live like this anymore. I took everything that was hers in the closet and packed it in her car. I grabbed everything that was in the drawers that was hers and also packed it into her car. There was no way we were working through this. If she wasn't done, I damn sure was. Once her car was packed, I took her house keys and locked my front door.

The police still hadn't arrived, so I got in the car and drove away. No sooner than I was five minutes away from the house, I saw the police speed past me, trying to get to my house. They didn't know I was the person they were coming for, so they continued to the house. I pulled the car over in the neighborhood and started to calm myself down, but instead all I could do was cry. My life was a mess. I loved this woman down to my soul and I couldn't believe she would hurt me in that manner.

I started to replay the events of what had happened over and over in my head. The more I did, the more I would cry—not because she had cheated, not because she had betrayed my trust, but because I realized that I had become the person I had hated the most as a child. I was Stanley and he was me.

"What have I done? What have I done?" I yelled while in the car.

I knew better. I wasn't raised to put my hands on any woman. There was never a reason for me to. Even if I was defending myself, I was strong enough to hold her until she calmed down. That was the only force I needed, but I'd literally swung on her like she was a man on the street. This was the woman I wanted to spend the rest of my life with. The woman who made me feel like no other, and I had disrespected her, our children, and our family like no other.

Later that night, I entered an empty house and walked around. I went into the bathroom to wash my face. And when I looked in the mirror, I no longer recognized the man that stood before me. I no longer respected the man I saw. All I saw was a man who had allowed his temper and emotions to get the best of him. I had allowed the devil and the world to interfere with what God had planned for me.

This wasn't me and today, it was going to stop. I might not ever get Lena back and that would be something I would have to live with for the rest of my life. I had to accept that, but what I didn't have to accept was the man I'd become. I wasn't going to accept that. I wasn't Stanley or any other abusive man or woman. I was Harold L. Turley II and I controlled my life. I quickly dropped down to my knees and prayed. I asked God for the strength to deal with this situation and for His help to overcome it.

CHAPTER 4

DOMESTIC VIOLENCE AND DOMESTIC ABUSE

D omestic abuse, also known as spousal abuse, occurs when one person in an intimate relationship or marriage tries to dominate and control the other person. An abuser doesn't "play fair." He or she uses fear, guilt, shame, and intimidation to wear you down and gain complete power over you. He or she may threaten you, hurt you, or hurt those around you. Domestic abuse that includes physical violence is called domestic violence.

Victims of domestic abuse or domestic violence may be men or women. Although studies say women are more commonly victimized, I tend to disagree. I believe when it occurs by a woman, it does tend to be overlooked or not looked at as domestic violence or abuse. How many times have you seen a woman smack a man and think nothing of it? That is domestic violence. Maybe you see her belittling her man; that is a part of domestic abuse. This happens day in and day out, but it's not perceived as a problem.

Am I pointing fingers toward women? No! I'm pointing the finger toward an abuser. Abuse can happen among heterosexual couples and in same-sex partnerships. Except for the gender difference, domestic abuse doesn't discriminate. It happens in all age ranges, ethnic backgrounds, and financial levels. I'll say that again—domestic abuse doesn't discriminate. It can happen at any stage of a relationship. It can be during a relationship, while the couple is breaking up, or even after the relationship has ended.

Despite what many people may believe, domestic violence isn't always due to the abuser's loss of control over their behavior. In fact, the violence inflicted usually is a deliberate choice made by the abuser in order to take control over their spouse or partner. Some even suggest that domestic violence is never due to an abuser's loss of control. I, too, disagree with this as well. I don't believe you can put abuse in a box and label it. I think every situation is different and due to this, different reactions are the cause.

Look at my situation. Yes, I chose to put my hands on Lena. I made the choice to punch her, a decision that I wasn't proud of. But if I told you that my anger and hurt from what was going on and what had happened in previous relationships caused it, I would be lying. Does this mean, whenever I get upset I'm going to react in that manner? No. In my case, the accumulation of events without me ever seeking help and learning how to expunge my anger led up to it. I compare it to a volcanic eruption. Is this an excuse for abuse? My answer is no! There is never an excuse or reason for anyone to commit abuse against their spouse or partner. However, there are reasons that lead to the abuse, and if you can recognize these reasons or symptoms prior to anything escalating, you can possibly avoid committing abuse against someone. That is my intent. Now let's look at some situations. We know an abuser's behavior isn't about anger or rage:

■ *Do you go around battering other individuals when you are upset? Or are these measures only restricted to your partner?*

We have all been in situations where someone has upset us or pissed us off outside of our spouse or partner. How did you react in that situation? When your boss passed you over for that promotion and gave it to someone who was less tenured and less qualified, did you go into your boss's office and beat the crap out of them? It's safe to assume this is an emphatic *no*. You were able to control your anger and rage. But yet, when your spouse or partner upsets you, you aren't able to control it. You can't help yourself. In this situation, I do not believe anger or rage is your reason. Now, it could be due to built-up anger and rage that was never addressed, but if you are battering your spouse repeatedly and blaming it on the fact that they upset you, that is an excuse. It's mirror time. Is this you?

■ *While you are having one of your episodes of rage or anger, do you stop when the phone rings or are you still furious when the police come knocking on the door?*

I can remember once as a child my neighbor, Mr. Clark, came home early and found his wife cheating. I don't know what happened when he walked into the house or what he actually saw, but I could only imagine. We all were outside waiting to see how things would play out. I remember Mr. Clark chasing the guy out of the house and catching him when he tried to get into his car. Mr. Clark hit him over and over again. He even picked up a stick and continued to beat him.

Once the police arrived, he didn't stop. He continued to beat this man over and over again for sleeping with his wife. He was in a fit of rage. It didn't matter who was around. It didn't matter who saw; his primary focus was the guy who was sleeping with his wife. That is a perfect example of rage. If when the phone rings or the police come knocking, and you act as if nothing has happened and you are calm and collected, that is not a fit of rage. It is the excuse you are using for your actions. Yes, you might have been upset or hurt, but you could control yourself. You could have chosen another way to handle the situation. You chose not to. Is this you?

■ *Abuse generally starts out as pushing or shoving, then escalates to hitting. Do you make sure to hit your spouse or partner in places where bruises or marks do not show?*

Mr. Clark wasn't aiming his punches. He wasn't trying to hide them or anything. The bottom line was Mr. Clark didn't care who saw what on the guy. His main purpose was to hurt him. Control wasn't even in his mindset. Remember an abuser's main focus is to dominate or control his partner. If you are out of control or in a rage, you won't be able to direct or limit where your kicks or punches land. You will be throwing them at will with no regard.

During my last encounter with Lena, I had snapped. When I had punched her, I wasn't trying to hit her in a place where it would be hidden. I didn't try to pinpoint my punch. I was frustrated and simply swung. And even in my fit of rage, I could have controlled it. I could have done something differently than what I did. I had made the choice to swing. Now if I can admit my fault, if I can admit that it could have been avoided, you can look in that mirror and be honest with yourself regarding your actions.

This isn't hard to know if this is you. Again, I'm not one to judge. I've made as many mistakes in my life as the next man. However, if this is you, you have a problem and it is not your temper. You are doing things in a manner not to get caught. You know what you are doing is wrong. You know exactly what you are doing to your spouse or partner. Please, please, please…Get help. Stop now! Seek a therapist who will help you find the source of your anger and deal with it. Your partner isn't the cause of it. However, you have made the choice to take it out on him or her. Please, stop and get help!

Now there are many signs if you are in an abusive relationship. This is whether you are the abuser or the one being abused. The most significant sign is fear. Does your spouse or partner fear you? Do you fear your spouse or partner? That's the first question you should ask yourself right now. Other signs include a partner who belittles you or tries to control you, and feelings of self-loathing, helplessness, and desperation.

To determine whether your relationship is abusive, answer the following questions. The more "yes" answers, the more likely it is that you are in an abusive relationship.

ABUSER

- Do you humiliate, criticize, or yell at your spouse or partner?
- Do you ignore or put down your spouse's or partner's opinions or accomplishments?
- Do you blame your spouse or partner for your abusive behavior?
- Do you see your spouse or partner as property or a sex object, rather than as a person?
- Do you have a bad and unpredictable temper?
- Do you hurt, or threaten to hurt or kill your spouse or partner? Regardless of your intent. This goes for if you mean what you are saying or only saying it as a form of intimidation. Both apply in this situation.
- Do you threaten to commit suicide if your partner or spouse says they are leaving you or if they actually do leave you?
- Do you force your spouse or partner to have sex with you?
- Do you destroy your belongings or your spouse's or partner's belongings?
- Do you act excessively jealous or possessive?
- Do you control where your spouse or partner goes or what they do?
- Do you keep your spouse or partner from seeing their friends or family?

- Do you limit access to money, the phone, or the car to your spouse or partner?
- Do you constantly check up or call your spouse or partner to see what they are doing or their whereabouts?

ABUSED

- Do you feel afraid of your spouse or partner much of the time?
- Do you avoid certain topics out of fear of angering your partner?
- Do you feel that you can't do anything right for your partner?
- Do you believe that you deserve to be hurt or mistreated?
- Do you wonder if you're the one who is crazy?
- Do you feel emotionally numb or helpless?

Remember, the truth hurts. You might be able to fool everyone within your circle, but you can't fool yourself. You can try to lie to yourself all you want, but what good will that do? This is about getting help. In order for you to be able to do that, you have to first accept responsibility for your actions. When reviewing the checklist, saying "that isn't me" or "I didn't do that" or "she doesn't do this" or "he doesn't do that," when you know that isn't the case isn't going to help your situation. Denial is the hardest thing to get over but the most necessary step for someone who truly wants to change and seek help. You cannot remain in denial. James 1:19-27 (NIV) reads:

> *My dear brothers, take note of this: Everyone should be quick to listen, slow to speak and slow to become angry, for man's anger does not bring about the righteous life that God desires. Therefore, get rid of all moral filth and the evil that is so*

prevalent and humbly accept the word planned in you, which
can save you.

Do not merely listen to the word, and so deceive yourselves.
Do what it says. Anyone who listens to the word but does not
do what it says is like a man who looks at his face in a mirror
and, after looking at himself, goes away and immediately for-
gets what he looks like. But the man who looks intently into the
perfect law that gives freedom, and continues to do this, not
forgetting what he has heard, but doing it—he will be blessed
in what he does.

If anyone considers himself religious and yet does not keep a
tight rein on his tongue, he deceives himself and his religion is
worthless. Religion that God our father accepts as pure and fault-
less is this: to look after orphans and widows in their distress
and to keep oneself from being polluted by the world.

Let's discuss this passage. It goes hand in hand with the message.
As with most topics in this book, I'll use myself and my life as a
prime example. I didn't know how to be quick to listen, slow to
speak and slow to become angry. Every little thing Lena said when
I asked a question, angered me. Instead of listening to what she
said, I listened to pieces of what she said and reacted to them.

Don't be so quick to have a reply. When confronting your
spouse or partner regarding an issue in your relationship or any
issue, take the time to listen to what is being said to you. Maybe
if you listen openly and without prejudgments, you will see his or
her side to the situation. I didn't do this in any situation.

Then to top if off, I allowed my anger to change myself from
the man I saw in the mirror day after day. I allowed my anger,
resentment, and bitterness from my past and my present to transform me into something I wasn't. I allowed it to transform me

into a man that I despised and hated. But yet, I saw this and could have stopped it. However, I made excuses for what I saw. I knew what I had become. Instead of owning up to it, accepting it, and changing it, I lied to the one person who could've helped me in that situation: myself.

Prime examples of this are in the story, *Round One* and *Round Two*. After I put my hands on Lena, I made excuses for why I choked her. There was no excuse for my actions. She hadn't done anything different than what she'd done in the past, and even if she had, I was still in a position to walk away. However, I chose not to. I often told myself I wouldn't have reacted a certain way if she hadn't pushed me or that her actions made me do what I did. This was her fault. I was very quick to shift the blame.

I was in denial about what I had become. It wasn't until in *The Final Round* where matters had escalated and I actually physically hit Lena, that I saw the true nature of the situation. Remember, I said pushing and shoving usually escalates to hitting. It's a cycle. Had I not been in denial, I possibly could have avoided what happened in *Round Two* and definitely *The Final Round*.

Just as I did, you also have the choice in every matter within your life. Even if you are dealing with rage, you still have a choice to seek help for your temper and find other ways to channel it. Now there is nothing that can be done when you are in one of your fits of rage. This is why you have to handle it before it gets to that point. I'm taking away any and every possible excuse you might give. There aren't many that I haven't either said or heard myself. Today, right now while reading this, let's vow to stop the excuses.

My grandmother once told me that excuses are nothing but examples of a man's incompetence, insecurities, and his ignorance. I no longer have any more excuses for my actions. I have learned to accept the fact that I had the choice in every matter. I made the wrong choice. Today, I ask you, will you stop making the wrong choices within your life? Today, will you look in the mirror and be honest with yourself with what you see? Today, will you change?

Just because you have entered the door of transformation into an abusive person, doesn't mean you have to stay in this room. A door has two purposes. One is to enter a room, the other is to exit. You aren't restricted to stay within this dark place. If you do, it's because you choose to. The main purpose for me writing this book is to show you that you aren't alone. I was you. The same demons you are facing, I had to face. The same position you are in right now, I, too, was once in that position.

The reality of this matter is if you do not get help, you will continue to hurt your spouse or partner, or someone else if your spouse or partner decides to leave. Do not think that this behavior is only isolated for a specific person. You will be surprised to find out that this behavior is isolated within you. So that means, regardless of who you are with, the same traits and behavior will resurface.

Are you ready to exit? Are you ready to be able to look at yourself in the mirror again and be proud of what you see? Are you ready to come from the shadows and into the sunlight? Is today the day? Will you make today your day? Not for your wife, not for your husband, not for your child, but for yourself. Will you make today the day you decide to exit from the abusive person you have become and transform into the person Christ designed for you to be?

Okay, let's see how well you have been paying attention. Do you remember what the first thing was I did when I realized the man I'd become and I decided to change? I got down on my knees and prayed. I repeatedly told you that you are not alone. Let's both pray together. If you are not of my faith, then I'll pray for you.

Heavenly Father,

We come to You in this time of despair in need of strength. We know that through You strength is made perfect in weakness, so we pray to You, give us the strength we need to recover from the shadows of the illness that has manifested within our body. Our body and mind have grown weary. Please renew our strength so we can seek the help we need in order to transform into the man or the woman free of abusive traits, free of abusive thoughts and free from abusive actions.

You have said that to Your children who have no might, You will increase their strength. We come to You today weak, we come to You today broken, and we come to You today lost. Bless us with a measure of strength, as may be sufficient for the task we have at hand.

When tempted by evil, deliver us, by granting us the power to overcome it. We know the path ahead of us isn't going to be an easy one. We know there will be stumbling blocks along the way as the devil tries to intervene. Give us Lord the strength to be able to handle any obstacle that may come our way, trying to impede our walk down the path of recovery.

If the burdens and stresses of the world try to oppress us beyond our bearings, please lighten our load so that our strength may be equal to it. We know that through Your grace and will, all things are possible. In Jesus' name we pray,

Amen

4th Stage
TRANSFORMATION (EXIT)

TO CHANGE IN CHARACTER OR CONDITION

Exit

1. A departure from a stage

2. The act of going out or going away

3. A way out of an enclosed place or space

CHAPTER 1

AM I ABUSIVE ?

How many of us have been to church, and at the end of the pastor's sermon, he opens the doors of the church and invites anyone to join or give their life to Christ? Well, just as the pastor extends the invitation and opens the doors of the church, I am offering you a similar invitation. I'm offering you the invitation to exit the door of abuse and transform yourself into the man or woman you were meant to be. Please, get up and go to your mirror one last time. Look at yourself long and hard and be honest. Do not lie to yourself anymore.

Ask yourself, "Am I abusive?" How many of the signs and symptoms of abuse, whether emotional, economic, or physical do I possess? If your answer is one or more, then you are abusive and need to seek help. Maybe you still question the signs and symptoms and are unclear about them. As you have read each story of what happened to me in my life, did you see yourself in any part of any story? Do you have to be in total control over your relationship? If your answer is yes, you are abusive. If you are in denial or this doesn't apply to you, then you might as well stop reading now. However, if you are ready to take that first step and say, "I am abusive and I am ready to get help," then please continue.

Congratulations! Now I want you to relax and take a deep breath. Exhale all that you have built up inside of you. If you are crying, do not feel ashamed. There is no need to wipe away your tears. It is okay, just let it out. There is nothing wrong with cleansing your soul. Today, you have taken a big step that is going to better your future. You were able to see that some, or maybe even all, of your actions and attitudes toward your spouse or partner are abusive. This is a huge step. It is perfectly natural to be emotional after such a discovery.

Now we have established that you realize this book pertains to you and your life. Let me be the first to say that I am proud of you. It might be a long time before you hear these words again. It takes a big person to admit their wrongs and seek help. Admitting you have a problem is the first step, but it is also the hardest. Making excuses for your actions is so easy to do. It is human nature to want to point the blame at someone else. Rarely do we want to face the wrong that we have done or inflicted upon others. Today, you have and I take my hat off to you.

By doing so, you have taken a very important step toward changing and being able to enjoy a mutually beneficial relationship. You have taken a part of yourself back and opened the door that will allow you to exit the man or woman you *used* to be. Well done! Acknowledging to ourselves that we have a problem, or that we are hurting someone we love is very, very difficult and painful, and many people can never quite admit it to themselves.

I cannot express how happy I am that I was able to get through to you with this book. I'm glad the message didn't escape you. I'm glad today you have decided to take a stand. I'm glad today you have decided to bring change into your life. I have accepted that I won't be able to reach everyone. To the people who I wasn't able to reach and have fallen by the wayside, my heart cries out to you. I pray that one day you will come to the realization that you have a problem and you need help.

Now for those who are ready to get help, if you are anything like me, you are probably beating yourself up wishing you can take back all the pain you have caused your spouse or partner. Let me be the first to tell you, there is nothing that you can do about the pain you have already caused. We can never get time back, but what we can do is take this time to change our ways to avoid it from happening in the future. Remember, regrets are nothing but mistakes not learned from. Just as I don't have any, I don't want you to have any regrets, either. Today, you start to make a difference in your own life. Instead of controlling your partner, you have taken control of what was needed: YOURSELF and your actions.

Now, the next step is to actually do the work in order to bring change within your life. I'm glad that you have admitted that you are abusive to yourself. However, do not be fooled in believing that will be enough or that will suffice. No, admitting you have a problem but not getting any help with that problem is like having faith in Christ but not doing your part with your actions on that faith. Yes, I said it. Just because you believe and have faith doesn't mean you stop there. No, your actions also need to demonstrate that faith.

James 2:14-17 (NIV) reads:

> *What good is it, my brothers, if a man claims to have faith but has no deeds? Can such faith save him? Suppose a brother or sister is without clothes and daily food. If one of you says to him, "Go, I wish you well; keep warm and well fed," but does nothing about his physical needs, what good is it? In the same way, faith by itself, if it is not accompanied by action, is dead.*

In this passage, James's point is that our actions mature our faith, even as faith motivates our actions. You have to allow your actions to mature your decision to get help and stop being abusive. How can you treat something when you don't even know the origin? I surely didn't. After I put my hands on Lena and decided to get help, the only thing I thought about is how I could have done what I did.

At that time, I still hated Stanley for what I saw him do to my mother. I hated him for what he did to me. Never would that be me. But in fact it was. What I saw as a child gave me the perception of what I thought a relationship was supposed to be, what a man's role was within the household and also the importance of respect. It was only after going to therapy that my therapist was able to discover the root of my problem. Key word, my "therapist" discovered the root to my problem, not me.

A lot of you might view therapy or counseling as a crutch. You might see it as something a weak-minded individual needs and you don't. Some might see it as a waste of time altogether. You might be telling yourself, "What do I look like, sitting down and telling some stranger my business? That isn't me. I can handle it by myself." Let me tell you this then, getting help and talking to a therapist shows how strong willed you really are. It takes a very strong individual to seek help from others. I know this from experience. I'm far from weak-minded, and therapy was nothing but a blessing for me, not a waste of time. Without it, I would have never uncovered the things I needed to in order to stop being abusive, and neither will you. You wouldn't attempt to put a Band-Aid over a gunshot wound, so don't try to patch this situation, either.

A lot of abusive behaviors are ingrained. They may have been a part of your personality and coping mechanism since childhood, and they are not easily recognized or cracked. Please do not try to diagnose yourself. This is going to be a long, tedious road to recovery. There is no quick fix. You have to be dedicated to your decision to change. Within therapy, you will find out a lot about yourself and your past. But more importantly, you will face the issues that are deep within you. Nobody can do this for you; you have to do for yourself. Are you ready? Are you ready to strap up those boots, dig in those heels and get to work? Great, now let's get to work!

CHAPTER 2

IT'S MY RESPONSIBILITY

I'm glad you have decided to get help. What you've told yourself is, I have a problem and I'm going to do whatever is needed to get help with that problem. This isn't going to be easy. The road to recovery is a long and tough road. It's going to take time, energy, and dedication. You cannot half-ass this because you will only get out of it what you put in it. If you deposit five dollars, guess how much you can withdraw? That's right, five dollars.

This means you need to put 110 percent of your effort into changing and doing all that you need to do in order to change. No one starts on a journey without a map. It's time you map out your plan to accomplish the challenge ahead of you. Everyone goes about this differently, but regardless of how you do it, it is your responsibility to map out your plan. It will be your responsibility to see it all the way through. In this chapter, I have included the five keys to my successful road to recovery.

It is not mandatory that you follow them in the order that I have written. Again, what works for one doesn't always work for the other. However, I do strongly advise that regardless of what map you design, make sure you include these five keys. They are the minimum. If you decide to add more, that is fine, but make sure these bases are covered.

BUILD A SUPPORTIVE TEAM

I'm going to start this out by going straight to scripture. Proverbs 20:18 reads: *Make plans by seeking advice; if you wage war, obtain guidance.* I cannot stress enough how hard dealing with overcoming your abusive ways is going to be. This is a war. There are going to be times when you want to quit. There are going to be times when you are in denial about things you discovery about yourself during your therapy sessions. There are going to be so many roadblocks and speed bumps that arise during this time. The devil wants to keep you in a state of confusion.

We all need that special someone who we can go to and talk. Yes, you have your therapist but you aren't going to have your therapist available to you twenty-four hours a day, seven days a week. Once you finish your session, you have to wait until your next scheduled appointment before you see your therapist again. In my case, I had weekly Monday appointments and they were only for an hour and a half. Whatever we couldn't cover within that time slot didn't get discussed until my next appointment.

You are not always going to be able to wait that long. Problems arise every day. I had to find someone who I could talk to throughout the week. I needed a supportive team to help me and be there for me throughout this journey. You will also. My suggestion to you is to find people who are unbiased and have your best interests at heart. Family and friends are fine but be careful and choose wisely. Just as family and friends can be a blessing, they can also be a burden. Everyone doesn't need to know your business. Only a select few do and I'm sure you already know who you can and can't trust. Follow your instincts and intuition when making your decision. Usually, it doesn't steer you wrong.

A good example of a bad choice is when I chose my mother once to confide in. Regardless of anything we have experienced, I love her to death and she is one of my closest friends. However, my mother isn't always the best person to turn to for advice. I knew this, so when I thought of who I could turn to, I made sure she wasn't one of them. Am I saying your mom isn't your best choice? No, I am not. I do not know what type of relationship you and your mother have, so I can't make that assumption. In the case of my mother, she couldn't be unbiased in every situation. I am my mother's child and when I'm hurt emotionally or physically, my mother thinks as my mother and not as my friend. Her opinion is no longer biased. It's centered on my pain. That isn't what I needed and if your mother is the same way, it's not what you need, either.

My supportive team consisted of my church counselor (a reverend at my church), my cousin, and my best friend. Why did I choose these three individuals? Simple, my best friend knew me like no other. My best friend had a proven track record of being honest with me when I was wrong, telling me things I didn't want to hear and putting me in my place if I needed it. Those were the exact qualifications I was looking for. I didn't need anyone who was going to further complicate things by agreeing with my denial or removing the finger that was pointing the blame at me. I needed someone that was going to say, "Why did you do this in that situation? Your therapist is right. You need to do this, that, and this, even though you don't want to, but it's what necessary." I needed someone to be stern with me, not because they were spiteful or trying to punish me but because it is what I needed. And finally I needed someone who was going to give great advice. My best friend fit the bill to the T.

I chose my cousin because just like my best friends, she knew me inside and out. She could reach me in a manner that no other person could. She had the gift to get me to see the other person's side without me getting defensive. She would put it in a manner that made perfect sense. Lastly, she had already gone through all that I had. She'd be on both sides of the abusive fence. Who better to turn to? She had already traveled down my road. She would know exactly what I needed and didn't need. She knew exactly what I was feeling and she knew how to conquer it. She was my success story. She was my proof that I could change. She was my hope. She was the light at the end of the tunnel that I was striving to reach. If she could turn her life around and turn her negative situation into a positive one, why couldn't I?

Finally, I chose someone within my church ministry for spiritual guidance along this journey. The way I looked at it, mentally I was sick. Where do people usually go when they are sick? They go to doctors or to a hospital. The church was my hospital. Christ has been in the healing business for over two thousand years. His track record speaks for itself. I wanted the best and He was waiting for me with open arms and steered me to exactly who I needed.

It turned out that my Reverend also dealt with domestic abuse. He had been abused as a child and the anger, resentment, and bitterness from that had manifested within him as well. He had also abused someone else because of this. The first thing he ever told me was that he didn't go through that situation for himself. Christ took him through that situation, so he could be an example to me of how to overcome it. I found it ironic because I always had questioned why Christ took me through all that I'd been through in my life and in that instance, I had my answer. I didn't go through all that I did for myself only. I went through it as well, to be *your* example of how *you* can overcome this.

FIND A LICENSED THERAPIST

Building a good supportive team was the first thing I did. Next I looked for the right therapist for me. You, too, are going to need to find a therapist who will be able to help you find the root of your problem. The therapist also can give you techniques and ways to better deal with situations that will arise in future relationships and in life. The selection process isn't always an easy task. There is no formula that I can give you about how to find a therapist.

My first suggestion would be look through your phonebook or online. Maybe your job has some type of program where they can refer you to talk to a therapist if you are dealing with stress, depression, or drug and alcohol abuse. Also, you can talk to your primary physician and ask him or her for a referral. Regardless of what option you choose, make sure you get the name and contact information for more than one therapist. This is for your development. You do not have to stick with your first choice, if you don't feel comfortable with that person. I called five and briefly asked questions about all of them during my initial calls. Ultimately, I felt comfortable with one.

I do not have that much experience with therapists, so I can't tell you everything that you should look for. However, I will say that when I chose my therapist, I felt confident with her ability. Some may have a racial or gender preference. Some may even have an age preference. The end result is it's your preference. Whatever makes you feel comfortable is what you need to seek.

Personally, I wanted a female therapist. My rationale was that my problems started and ended with a woman. I was introduced to abuse by my mother and realized I was abused and abusive with Lena. I didn't know a lot, but who better to know women's tendencies and give me an honest opinion regarding their behavior and my subsequent reactions than another woman? I also wanted an older woman, preferably someone in her late forties or early fifties. Race didn't matter to me.

My therapist ended up being an older white woman who practiced with her husband. It wasn't long before I was talking to both of them together. They were in their sixties and such a blessing because I got both sides. I was able to get the woman's perspective, and her husband was able to give me his professional advice about what worked for him in their own relationship. They were the perfect team, for me! You have to find your perfect team, whether it's a tandem or a single therapist.

You might ask...how will a therapist be able to help me? That is a great question. A therapist will be able to help control you saying something hurtful or doing something harmful to your spouse or partner. They will be able to help you recognize your reactions within yourself. They will be able to help you deal with how you feel when you get wound up or upset. Sounds simple and easy, right? Well, it's not. Please do not think you can do this yourself or handle this with someone in your supportive group.

You might be blessed as I was to have someone in your supportive group who has gone through what you are going through. They might be able to share with you, what helped them get over their situation. But you always have to keep in mind that, that was *their* situation and not yours. Each is different. What helped them doesn't mean it will automatically help you. They are a part of your supportive team to provide you with support—not to diagnose your condition and help you solve it. Please do not mix the two.

Now, with anything, someone has to be hard-headed and do things their own way before they learn that their way isn't the right way. If that is you, please take this test first to see that you need help. You can not go at this alone. Ask yourself these questions and more importantly, be honest with yourself. You can fool me, but this isn't about me. This is about you.

- Do you now or did you in the past regularly vent your frustration on your partner?
- Do you tell yourself that your partner is overreacting to "being told off"?

- Do you tell yourself what you do is not that bad, so-and-so would be far worse or so-and-so does this?
- Do you think that if your partner didn't do things that got you upset on purpose, then the abuse would not happen in the first place?
- Do you tell yourself that your partner deserved the abuse because of what they did to you or how they treated you?
- Do you tell yourself that because you only get nasty when you are drunk or high, it isn't really the same as if you were really abusive?

If you answered YES to any of the above questions—it doesn't matter if it was one, two, three or more—then you still are not taking full responsibility for your actions. You never will until you get professional help. You need to find out the original source of your problem if you are ever going to be able to conquer it. Talking to a therapist doesn't show signs of weakness, but rather shows how strong you are to know that you can't do it by yourself.

PRACTICE WHAT YOU ARE TAUGHT

What good is getting help if you don't apply what you have been taught in your everyday walk of life? It's useless and wasted if you don't. I don't know about you, but I'm not a big fan of doing things half-assed, as my mother would say. If I commit to changing, I'm going to commit 150 percent to change. For myself, instead of expressing what bothers me, I tend to keep it bottled up inside of me. I know I shouldn't keep it within me. I know I should get it off my chest and talk about it; however, I don't. I hold it and hold it and hold it.

During my sessions, I learned that no matter how long I try to hold whatever is bothering me, sooner or later, it will come out in one form or another. It's just as if you drink glass after glass of water; sooner or later, you are going to have to use the bathroom. The longer you hold it, the worse it will be. That anger and pain has to be discarded, not stored. I learned it is fine for me to vent when I'm upset. It is a natural reaction for me to get upset or angry. I just can't hold onto those feelings. I have to discard them. I wasn't doing that, though. I was holding on to the anger allowing it to build up within me. The more I held on to it, the more the bitterness built within my spirit.

Another thing I had to learn is that every issue isn't worth fighting for or arguing about. My partner could never understand why the smallest thing she would do would possibly hurt me. I'm generally a very laid-back and fun-loving guy. People who are within my inner circle will attest to this. I'm always joking and trying to keep everyone's spirit up. I rarely allow anyone to steal my joy. Shoot, I figure smiling is free and so is happiness, so why should I allow someone to steal the one thing I don't have to pay for?

People always try to get under your skin or pluck your nerves and generally, I won't allow them to with me. I'll debate with you all day long, but I'm not about to sit here and get mad over it. Either we can agree to disagree or you can keep it moving; you can choose. I don't care which you choose. That is simply my philosophy the majority of the time.

This same way of thinking and laid-back attitude wasn't the case when it came to my partner. She could never understand why. Shoot, even I couldn't after a while. A part of me felt like I was acting out of character. Maybe I was oversensitive when it came to her. But then I had to realize my feelings for this woman versus anyone else. I loved this woman. I still to this day love her wholeheartedly. The reason why she could do or say the same thing someone else did—and it bothered me—was because of how much I loved her. There was no shield with her. Anyone else, I didn't care about them or their opinion didn't matter, so whatever they said didn't bother me. Her opinion mattered. Her words could cut like the sharpest knife and wound my soul.

Because of this, I would argue her down, trying to prove whatever point it was. I would verbally fight with her, no matter what. That was a very slippery slope I traveled down. Proverbs 17:14 states: *Starting a quarrel is like breaching a dam; so drop the matter before a dispute breaks out.*

Keep this in mind because the minute you open the flood gates to an argument, you never know where it's going to lead or if you can come back from it. Is your relationship really worth that risk? Mine wasn't. Recalling the majority of what we argued about, if we would have listened to each other, none of them would have been issues or problems, which leads me to my next point.

UNDERSTAND THE DIFFERENCE BETWEEN AN ARGUMENT AND A DISAGREEMENT

I love a good discussion. Communication is the key to every successful and healthy relationship. If you can not talk to your spouse or partner, the chances of that person remaining in your life under that capacity aren't good. Without communication, you have nothing. That is the foundation to any good relationship.

Would you build the base of your house from straw or would you prefer it be built from concrete? Communication is your concrete. The lack of it is your straw. Now let's assume the foundation is there, however, throughout the road of life the two of you stopped being able to communicate with each other. Your discussions and disagreements are nothing but arguments. All you do now is argue time and time again.

I'm sure we all have been in this situation. If you haven't, then I don't know how you were able to get so far along within this book because it is not for you. No one enjoys constant arguments. After a while they will start to weigh on you. This is correctable if you understand the difference between a disagreement and an argument.

The reason why arguments escalate and nothing is accomplished in an argument is because your main objective is to convince the other person your view is the correct one. That isn't healthy. Even if you are right and the other person is wrong, the way you are going about it, your spouse or partner will never be able to see that. All you'll continue to do is argue and never see eye to eye. That in turn will only continue to divide the two of you.

Now a disagreement is something different. There is nothing wrong with disagreements. Actually, they are healthy and much needed in a relationship. The difference between a disagreement and an argument is that in a disagreement, each of you states your point and listens to the other's. The key word is "listen." It is no longer a right or wrong situation. It's about understanding each other and seeing how you and your spouse or partner came to whatever conclusion you have. If both of you can see the other's point, neither of you are upset. It's no confusion. Even if you don't agree with your spouse's or partner's point, they understand yours. You can always agree to disagree and keep it moving.

EVERYONE DOESN'T NEED TO KNOW YOUR BUSINESS

Finally, I started things off with *"Build your supportive team,"* so I have to make sure you understand that this doesn't mean everyone needs to know your business. Trust me, this is only going to bring and add more problems. You might have to learn this the hard way, as I did. I thought that by me discovering that the more I kept things inside myself, the more the bitterness grew, I vowed to always vent. I wasn't going to keep things bottled up inside of me anymore. That is what my therapist suggested. However, she never suggested talking to any and everyone about my situation, and that's what I was doing. I was telling too many people my business and personal information.

Let's go to scripture, Matthew 8:15-16 (NIV) that reads:

> *Watch out for false prophets. They come to you in sheep's clothing, but inwardly they are ferocious wolves. By their fruit you will recognize them. Do people pick grapes from thornbushes, or figs from thistles?*

Everyone is not your friend, neither do they have your best interest at heart. This goes for family, friends, and coworkers. It doesn't matter. You see, some people will bait you into you telling them your business for their own personal need. Some will bait you into it so they can gossip. There are so many different reasons why they will. You have your supportive team. You have who you can go to and talk to. Stick within that circle. It will save you less heartache in the long run.

After my last incident with Lena, I was so hurt and upset by my actions. I had to get it off my chest. Keep in mind, this was all before I first saw my therapist. Who was the first person I called? My mother. I didn't hide anything. I told her everything. I told her I put my hands on Lena. I told her about the affair between Lena and the other guy. I mean, I told her *everything* venting my anger and frustration and thinking my mother would give me sound advice on what to do. My spirit was broken. Sitting here today writing this, I can't help but laugh. I don't know what the hell I was thinking telling my mother. Nothing positive or useful would be accomplished by it.

Now mind you, ninety percent of the time my mother gives great advice, but I didn't factor in the subject. My mother was upset at Lena because she cheated. All my mother saw was that her son was hurt, not what her son did wrong in the situation. She didn't excuse my actions but that should have been her focus. That should have been her primary concern. It wasn't. My mother took it upon herself to call Lena and cuss her out for cheating on me.

By opening my mouth and venting to someone else, I made matters worse. How do you think Lena felt? I'm not sure what was said within the conversation, but can you imagine your spouse or partner hitting you and you being blamed for it? I can't imagine how she felt. That is like telling a rape victim it's her fault she was raped. Please, be careful who you talk to and share your business with. My mother didn't have bad intentions, but she handled the situation incorrectly. It was my fault because she shouldn't have even known what was going on. I should have never put her in my situation.

Now this was my mother—think if it was someone else. Think if it was a coworker or someone who I presumed to be my friend. I can only imagine the type of damage that could have done. Proverbs 20:19 (NIV) states: *A gossip betrays a confidence; so avoid a man who talks too much*. Keep your business just that, *your* business. It's no one else's.

Whew, now I've said a mouth full and a lot of it is much easier said than done. This is your life, though. This is your relationship. This is about taking responsibility to be a better man or woman and laying the foundation for your future. Taking responsibility for your actions doesn't only mean admitting that you were wrong with whatever you have done. Admitting is the first step within the process, but getting help and making sure you do not continue to repeat the abuse is the major part of taking responsibility for your actions.

CHAPTER 3

WILL GETTING HELP SAVE MY RELATIONSHIP?

I can't tell you how many emails I've received asking this very question. If I decide to get help, do you think it will save my relationship? If this is your purpose for getting help, then my answer is no. It will not save your relationship because you will not change. You are only getting help in an effort to keep your spouse or partner from leaving and not because you want to get help.

Now I know that although this should be the last of your worries, most of the time it's the first thing you think of. Common sense tells me you will try to do anything to get your spouse or partner back, especially if you truly loved that person. Dealing with a breakup can be the hardest thing to handle. I know. I lost the love of my life due to my actions so I completely understand.

I used the name "Lena" throughout this novel. However, the name "Lena" only signifies all the women I've dealt with in my life. There have been several women who have played the role of "Lena" in life. But the one who mattered the most to me, when I lost her, I felt like it was the end of the world. I couldn't see any light at the end of the tunnel. I'd prayed for a love like that and when I finally found it, I didn't appreciate it.

I was at a point in my life where I was done with all the non-sense of being single. I didn't need the clubs. I didn't need other women. I had finally found the one woman who completed me. We built a solid foundation from the start. She was my best friend.

In essence, she meant the world to me and I felt as if I was nothing without her.

When she walked out of that front door, my first thought was what had I done? What had I become? I no longer knew who I was anymore. I no longer respected the man I saw before me whenever I looked into the mirror and that was unacceptable. No woman could love me if I didn't love myself. In each of these sentences, you see the word "I" and not her. My primary focus was on *me*.

Rebuilding *me* became my goal and my inspiration. Yes, I was heartbroken and battled depression when we broke up. But I got help for myself. I got help because I wanted to be the man my children looked up to, the man my grandmother and mother raised me to be, and more importantly, the man who the Lord wanted me to be. My life is a gift from God; what I do with my life is my gift to Him.

If your primary goal for getting help is to save your relationship, your motives are misplaced. However, I'm not slow or stupid. I know this is on your mind. My only advice is to find a way to get it off your mind. Your focus right now should not be on the relations you are in, the relationship you have lost, or the person who you have hurt. Your primary focus right now should be on yourself. You are the one who needs to get help.

Your spouse or partner needs to get help also to be able to deal with the abuse you have caused them, but that shouldn't be anywhere in your mind at this point. The only thing you should be thinking about is getting the help that you need to break the cycle of abuse you are causing and inflicting upon others. You should want to make a stand to say that hey, regardless of what my spouse or partner does, today the abuse stops within me.

For those of you who have the right motives regarding getting help, I know it's still in the back of your mind. You are still wondering hey, is it possible I will be able to save my relationship? My answer is, it may and it may not. I can't give you any statistics to say that hey, seventy-eight percent lose their spouse or partner or sixty-seven percent will try to work things out if their abusive partner gets help. These statistics *do not* exist. However, I can give you reality. By the time the abusive person realizes he or she has a problem, too much has already happened and the trust can not be rebuilt. Though it may pain you to read this and you don't want to hear it, that is the reality of the situation.

Let's go back to the ones who have misplaced motives. I know I don't gender discriminate within this book. However, this right now is for the men. Sadly, a lot of men will refer themselves to programs for help or seek out a therapist only in a bid to stop their partner from leaving or even in a bid to persuade her to come back and give it another try. If you are seeking help with this sole intention of keeping or regaining your spouse or partner who had decided to leave due to you being abusive, then you are doing this for the wrong reason. As I don't judge, I also will not sugarcoat the situation. You are doing this only as a tool to get or keep what you want. This tells me you haven't learned anything. You are still trying to control your situation instead of yourself.

I told you that there aren't any statistics regarding the ratio of how many people give an abusive person a second or third chance if they get help. Well, I do have one statistic for you. One hundred percent of people who do not seek change because they truly want to change, DO NOT CHANGE. They continue to be the same person. They are only trying to suppress the abusive traits. As with anything else suppressed, it will resurface eventually.

It doesn't matter if you try to con your spouse or partner by going to therapy. Therapy or counseling can really only help if *you* want to change. Unfortunately, you have to go into things thinking that you have lost the love of your life. He or she is not coming back regardless of if you seek help or if you have changed. They will never be able to trust you again. Now am I saying this is what is going to happen? No, I am not. It is possible your spouse or partner may forgive you, but you do not need to be thinking about that.

Concentrate on today and not tomorrow. We have all heard the saying tomorrow isn't promised to us so live today to its fullest, but let's also go to scripture on this.

Matthew 6:33-34 (NIV) reads:

> *But seek first his kingdom and his righteousness, and all these things will be given to you as well. Therefore do not worry about tomorrow, for tomorrow will worry about itself. Each day has enough trouble of its own.*

In other words, deal with the problems that face you today first before you try to handle tomorrow's problems. The problem you face today is more than enough for you to handle. We always want to look ahead first instead of handling the issue and then dealing with tomorrow's worries tomorrow.

Now I said I wouldn't push my spirituality on anyone and I'm going to hold firm with that. But notice the beginning of the text. *But seek first his kingdom and his righteousness, and all these things will be given to you as well.* What was the first thing I did after I looked in the mirror and vowed to change? I looked toward the Lord's kingdom for help. I prayed for His guidance to help me deal with the issue at hand. Regardless of whether you are Baptist, Catholic, Buddhist, Muslim or any other religion, you know who to seek first.

I know most of you are wondering did getting help save my relationship? You are patiently sitting and waiting for the happy ending that most books have. Well, this book is about life, my life and there is no happy ending for me to give you. You will be waiting a long time to hear what you are looking for. My decision to get help didn't save my relationship. The only thing that it saved was me. She couldn't bring herself to forgive me and honestly, I don't blame her. She put her trust in me and our relationship, and I hurt her.

Trust is the easiest thing to lose but the hardest thing to regain. You see, with the last person who played the role of "Lena" in my life, I'd never hurt her prior to hitting her. We had arguments from time to time and we were having problems. However, I hadn't done anything to lose her trust. After I got help, of course I tried to work things out. A part of me even felt like I was entitled to a second chance. This was the first time I'd made a mistake and though it was a very serious one, it was only one.

Well, in life, you aren't guaranteed a second chance. You are only guaranteed the first chance. Anything after the first one is a gift. It took me a long time to understand that. Am I stealing your hope? Are you now starting to second-guess getting help? I hope not because though I lost what mattered most to me, I regained myself. It's not an even trade or exchange but it was what Christ had intended for me.

Now that I've stolen your hope, I'll give you some. As I said, she was my best friend. We had a great foundation.

Matthew 7:24-27 (NIV) reads:

Therefore everyone who hears these words of mine and puts them into practice is like a wise man who built his house on the rock. The rain came down, the streams rose, and the winds blew and beat against that house; yet it did not fall, because it had its foundation on the rock. But everyone who hears these words of mine and does not put them into practice is like a foolish man who built his house on sand. The rain came down, the streams rose, and the winds blew and beat against that house, and it fell with a great crash.

Every relationship has its storms and seasons. If your relationship isn't built of rock, when the storm comes, it will crash down. We have gone through our storm. The rain and the wind crashed down hard, however, our foundation is still solid. We still communicate and, more importantly, we are still friends. I am a true believer that Christ, at times, has to remove something from our life in order for us to truly appreciate what He has given us.

Right now, we aren't together but does this mean that once He is finishing building her of rock she won't be back? No, it doesn't. I will not tell you if it's meant to be, it will be; that isn't always true. God gives us the choice. We don't always make the right decision or choice. That doesn't mean that it wasn't meant to be. It means that we didn't choose to do what was needed in order to be.

What I will say is that time can cure a lot of things. Concentrate on yourself and building yourself of rock, so that the next time a storm comes, you will stand tall in the midst of it. This might be your season to be apart. When the weather breaks and the next season comes around, maybe you'll appreciate it a little better than you did before. What do you think? I think so.

MOVING FORWARD

This is the finale of the book. It has been a long journey, a long road. I've opened up my life to each and every one of you. I have used my life as an example of what your life is, could be and doesn't have to be if you do not allow it to. Out of all that I have been through, what I am most proud of is that I can stand in front of you today and any day afterward and tell you that I have moved forward with my life. I have exited the door of abuse and transformed myself into a better person.

I no longer hold any resentment to anyone in my past. I am not bitter or angry. I'm at peace and trying to live a life full of happiness. I'm happy with the road God has taken me down. I don't question anything about my journey. I know that in life there are only two things ever promised to you. I was promised to live and to die. How long I have or anything else was never promised to me. Never was I sat down and promised that life would be easy. Life is filled with trials and tribulations.

I can remember as a young boy, one day after church I begged my grandmother if I could walk back to her house. I didn't want to ride back with her. I never told her my true reasoning for wanting to walk instead of ride with her, but she knew I was up to something. She agreed to allow me to walk home, but only under one condition: I was to go straight home and make no stops. If I wanted to be able to walk, I had no choice but to agree. I proceeded to my grandmother's house and the minute her car was out of sight, I sprinted to the corner store to buy some candy. It was on the way to Grandma's house. I figured if I ran to the store and got my candy, then ran the rest of the way to Grandma's, it would be as if I had walked and didn't make any stops.

I ran into the store, quickly ordered some bubble gum and Johnny Appleseeds and then sprinted to my grandmother's. I stopped about two houses before hers to catch my breath. When I walked into the house, Grandma was already in the kitchen preparing breakfast. I went and got a quick glass of water, then went upstairs to change my clothes. I knew I couldn't eat my candy yet. Grandma was much wiser than that, so I put it in my pocket and went back downstairs and waited for breakfast.

My plan was after breakfast, I'd ask if I could go out on the porch. Grandma never had a problem with me being on the porch. Once I was outside, I could finally have my candy. Once breakfast was finished, Grandma asked me to come into the kitchen. I didn't think anything of it but I should have known better. Grandma asked me to empty my pockets into the trash can. I looked at her, shocked, trying to figure out how she knew.

I protested. It wasn't fair. I'd bought the candy with my own money. Grandma had made it perfectly clear prior to her leaving church that I should come straight home. I was to make no stops and I didn't follow the rules. Upset, I threw my candy into the trash. I couldn't believe it. It wasn't fair.

Once time had passed and I'd cooled off, Grandma sat me down and let me know that throughout life, I will continue to make mistakes. "Life is filled with trouble, and all of us have to walk through some of those troubles," she said.

The store was my temptation, and I wasn't strong enough to resist that temptation. Instead of being honest with my grandmother from the beginning and telling her my reason for wanting to walk home in fear of her telling me no, I'd hide it. My actions had repercussions. Keep this story in mind when we talk about temptation along your road forward.

Though an abusive person might question all they've been through, this affected the abused person more. If you've been abused, you can not beat yourself up. The object is rebuilding yourself so that you can sustain a successful and meaningful relationship in the future. Don't question the road you have traveled because it was designed to be this way.

As my grandmother said, if there is one thing life is filled with it's trouble. All of us have to walk through those troubles. They can't be avoided. Some of us will have more trouble than others, but regardless of what we go through, God has it all under control. Do not concentrate on the negative that occurred during your troubled walk. Everything happened for a reason. Some difficulties teach patience. Some difficulties teach us to have compassion. Some difficulties teach gratitude. Some difficulties build character.

James 1:2-18 speaks toward trials and temptations. Let's break it down in sections. James 1:2-8 (NIV) reads:

> *Consider it pure joy, my brothers, whenever you face trials to many kinds, because you know that the testing of your faith develops perseverance. Perseverance must finish its work so that you may be mature and complete, not lacking anything. If any of you lacks wisdom, he should ask God, who gives generously to all without finding fault, and it will be given to him. But when he asks, he must believe and not doubt, because he who doubts is like a wave of the sea, blown and tossed by the wind. That man should not think he will receive anything from the Lord; he is a double-minded man, unstable in all he does.*

I can remember a friend of mine calling me once. She had just gone through a very bad breakup due to abuse. She'd left her man and had moved back in with her parents. There was really no room at their place for her, but she needed a place to lay her head until she could find her own place. She did what any strong woman would do, she made do.

She got an air mattress and she and her children slept on the floor. She called me one night distraught. She couldn't believe that the reality she was living was now her life. I didn't know what to tell her. I didn't know how to comfort her in that situation. Then it dawned on me. Christ had taken her through this experience because He was building something within her. However, I couldn't tell her what He was building. But I assured her that in time, Christ would show her and make it known exactly what He was building.

No one wants to be abused and if I could stop it from happening to anyone, please believe I would. However, I have to believe the trials we experience throughout life are for a reason. They were designed to build something within us that was lacking. Our faith was being tested to develop perseverance within us. A part of that test is having faith in Christ that He will pull you through. Do not be a "double-minded" person. A "double-minded" person is uncommitted and unstable, wavering between wholehearted trust in God and a worldly approach to life.

Now that you have survived your trial, also know that in moving forward there will be temptation to regress back to your former self. For some, this isn't an option as their will and faith in themselves is strong and unbreakable. But for others, you lack the faith needed within yourself and question how strong-willed you really are.

James 1:12-18 (NIV) reads:

> *Blessed is the man who preserves under trial, because when he stood the test, he will receive the crown of life that God has promised to those who love him.*
>
> *When tempted, no one should say, "God is tempting me." For God cannot be tempted by evil, nor does He tempt anyone; but each one is tempted when, by his own evil desire, he is dragged away and enticed. Then, after desire has conceived, it gives birth to sin; and sin, when it is full-grown, gives birth to death.*
>
> *Don't be deceived, my dear brothers. Every good and perfect gift is from above, coming down from the Father of the heavenly lights, who does not change life shifting shadows. He chose to give us birth through the word of truth, that we might be a kind of firstfruits of all he created.*

Remember in my story regarding my grandmother I told you about my temptation on the road to her house. Well, there will be temptation along your road to recovery. If you get angry easily, there will be people by design to try to upset you. This isn't God tempting you. God doesn't tempt with evil. But God does provide us "gifts" that confirm what we've learned. This means when you come home and you get upset with your spouse or partner but go into another room and calm down, then talk out your problem. You have just turned the devil's temptation into one of God's gifts.

Do you know it's an awesome feeling to have people come up to me or email me and say, "Thank you for telling my story... Thank you for helping me to see that I was abusive...Thank you for helping me to see that I am in an abusive relationship…Thanks for letting me know what I need to do in this situation…Thank you for allowing me to see my true self." It makes this book all worth while. It confirms for me that everything that I endured in my life wasn't for me but to potentially benefit millions of other people. I am proof that everything we go through in life can be worked out to our benefit and for our good, if we apply the lessons learned to our advantage instead of our disadvantage.

If you didn't capture everything expressed in this book, I want you to remember this. When you are looking in the mirror, it's you and only you. You do not have an audience. Stop lying to the one person who counts—you. Also remember, you have to forgive so that you can be forgiven. Do not continue to hold on to your anger or it will surely turn into bitterness.

Now that you're finished reading this book, I hope you have cried, I hope you have laughed, but more importantly, I hope you have learned what the effects of abuse can do or lead to. I hope I was able to awaken you to what you have been doing or what has been happening to you. I hope that I was successful in inspiring you to seek help. But more significantly, I hope that I can say you are on the same road as I am currently on. I hope we are traveling on the same interstate. I hope you are have stopped the abuse and are moving forward with your life!

ACKNOWLEDGMENTS

I will keep my acknowledgments very brief. First and foremost, I want to thank Christ for giving me the strength to tell my story. Writing this brought back a lot of painful memories. I know that you have a purpose with my life and you have given me the gift of being able to tell a story. You also gave me the strength to tell mine.

I want to thank my mother, Anna Stroman, and my father, Harold L. Turley Sr. Without either of you, there would be no me. Though neither one of you is perfect and have made mistakes along my life, the one thing that is unquestionable is your love for me. Without it, I would have been far worse than I can imagine.

I want to thank my grandmother, Lillian Milner, and my grandfather, DeArthur Milner. Though neither of you are here with me in the flesh, I always carry you around with me in my heart. You were the design of a perfect relationship. Not one without problems, but one with how to handle those problems and continue to love each other more and more each day. Grandma, you once told me never go to bed upset with my girlfriend or wife, and I told you I couldn't promise you that. Today I can. I understand why you said it and I make sure regardless of the situation or how upset I am, she knows I love her.

I want to thank my children, Harold L. Turley III (Tre), RaShawn Turley, Malik Brown, and Yhanae Turley. You are my definition of love. Because of you, I strive to be a better man each day. For my boys, I pray that you all become better men than I ever was; and for my baby girl, I pray that you marry a man who loves you more than Daddy loves you. For if he does, I know he will honor and cherish you forever.

I want to thank my brother, Jerome West, and my sister, Ashante James, for just being who you are. JD, though you often say you look up to me, you have never heard me say how proud I am of you and all that you do. I envy you on so many levels. You are my hero! Shante, we have to be the first set of twins nine years apart. You are so much like me it's scary, but I wouldn't trade that for anything in this world. I will always have your back and be your rock.

I want to thank my publisher, Zane, for believing in my vision and supporting my dream. You give me the avenue to share my gift with the world. There aren't many publishers who are kind-hearted to have patience with me as I take my time in between books, but there aren't many people in the world with your kind-hearted spirit and understanding. You are a true blessing.

To the hardest-working woman at Strebor, Charmaine, I want to thank you for all that you do. You stay on top of everything. I just wish I had a Charmaine in every aspect of my life.

I want to thank my Pastor, Delman Coates of Mt. Ennon Baptist Church. It wasn't long ago where I was lost within the world. I knew and accepted Jesus Christ as my Lord and Savior, however, I wasn't regular within my faith and walk. I wasn't attending church regularly because I hadn't found the right messenger who could reach me until I came to Mt. Ennon. I thank the Lord for blessing me with you.

I have to thank my supporting cast, Eddie Waddy, James Nunn, and Reggie Johnson. I thank all three of you brothers for different things but one common reason: your friendship. No matter the situation, no matter the time. When I need any of you, you are always there.

Though I have a HUGE family, and most of them will probably kill me after reading this and not seeing their name in print, I want to thank two in particular—Shamee Allen and Dytrea Langon. It's no secret I'm closest to both of you. Thank you for all the talks, all the support and loving me unconditionally. Thank you for making it known when I'm wrong and for the praise when I'm right. Thank you for being in my corner. I love you both dearly.

I want to thank Tomeka Turley and Candace Brown for your role in shaping me into the man I am today. Without either of you, I wouldn't be who I am today. I'd have less gray hair. LOL!

I saved this person for last because she means the most to me. I want to thank the woman who is my best friend, my companion, my lover and hopefully, one day my wife. You are a gift from God. You have taught me the true meaning of love, trust, and friendship. We have had our ups as well as our downs but through it all, whether next to me or from afar, you have always been by my side. I love you for all that you do and I love you even more for what you haven't done or will do in the future. You are the smile that is on my face when I wake up in the morning and the comfort that my heart feels when I go to bed. You are the reason why I strive to be a better man!

There are many more people who have influenced and shaped my life. I wish I could include each and every one of you but I cannot. Just know that you aren't forgotten and are definitely appreciated. Whether it be for a calming talk, providing me with a much needed laugh, or for just being a friend, I thank each and every one of you!

Finally, I have to thank my readers and fans. It feels weird to say fans, because I'm a fan of writing and for me to possibly have fans is unimaginable. Please know that you are my inspiration. I feel honored that you enjoy my work and pray you continue to read it. Thank you!

SCRIPTURE NOTES

Chapter 5: ANGER AND BITTERNESS, THE GOOD AND THE EVIL

PSALM 62 (NIV):

My soul finds rest in God alone; my salvation comes from him.

He alone is my rock and my salvation; he is my fortress, I will never be shaken.

How long will you assault a man?

Would all of you throw him down—this leaning wall, this tottering fence?

They fully intend to topple him from his lofty place; they take delight in lies.

With their mouths they bless, but in their hearts they curse.

Find rest, O my soul, in God alone; my hope comes from him.

He alone is my rock and my salvation; he is my fortress, I will not be shaken.

My salvation and my honor depend on God; he is my mighty rock, my refuge.

Trust in him at all times, O people; for God is our refuge.

Lowborn men are but a breath, the highborn are but a lie; if weighed on a balance, they are nothing; together they are only a breath.

Do not trust in extortion or take pride in stolen goods; though your riches increase, do not set your heart on them.

One thing God had spoken, two things have I heard; that you,

O God, are strong, and that you, O Lord, are loving surely you will reward each person according to what he has done.

1 Corinthians 13:4-13 (NIV):

Love is patient, love is kind. It does not envy, it does not boast, it is not proud. It is not rude, it is not self-seeking, it is not easily angered, it keeps no record of wrongs. Love does not delight in evil but rejoices with the truth. It always protects, always trusts, always hopes, always preserves.

Love never fails. But where there are prophecies, they will cease; where there are tongues, they will be stilled; where there is knowledge, it will pass away. For we know in part and we prophesy in part, but when perfection comes, the imperfect disappears. When I was a child, I talked like a child, I thought like a child, I reasoned like a child. When I became a man, I put childish ways behind me. Now we see but a poor reflection as in a mirror; then we shall see face to face. Now I know in part; then I shall know fully, even as I am full known.

And now these three remain: faith, hope and love. But the greatest of these is love.

Chapter 9: TOTAL CONTROL

2 Timothy 1:1-7 (NIV):

I thank God, whom I serve, as my forefathers did, with a clear conscience, as night and day I constantly remember you in my prayers. Recalling your tears, I long to see you, so that I may be filled with joy. I have been reminded of your sincere faith, which first lived in your grandmother Lois and in your mother Eunice and, I am persuaded, now lives in you also. For this reason I remind you to fan into flame the gift of God, which is in you through the laying on of my hands. For God did not give us a spirit of timidity, but a spirit of power, of love, and of self-discipline.

Chapter 14: DOMESTIC VIOLENCE AND DOMESTIC ABUSE

JAMES 1:19-27 (NIV):

My dear brothers, take note of this: Everyone should be quick to listen, slow to speak and slow to become angry, for man's anger does not bring about the righteous life that God desires. Therefore, get rid of all moral filth and the evil that is so prevalent and humbly accept the word planned in you, which can save you.

Do not merely listen to the word, and so deceive yourselves. Do what it says. Anyone who listens to the word but does not do what it says is like a man who looks at his face in a mirror and, after looking at himself, goes away and immediately forgets what he looks like. But the man who looks intently into the perfect law that gives freedom, and continues to do this, not forgetting what he has heard, but doing it, he will be blessed in what he does.

If anyone considers himself religious and yet does not keep a tight rein on his tongue, he deceives himself and his religion is worthless. Religion that God our father accepts as pure and faultless is to look after orphans and widows in their distress and to keep oneself from being polluted by the world.

Chapter 15: AM I ABUSIVE?

JAMES 2:14-17 (NIV):

What good is it, my brothers, if a man claims to have faith but has no deeds? Can such faith save him? Suppose a brother or sister is without clothes and daily food. If one of you says to him,

"Go, I wish you well; keep warm and well fed," but does nothing about his physical needs, what good is it? In the same way, faith by itself, if it is not accompanied by action, is dead.

Chapter 16: IT'S MY RESPONSIBILITY

PROVERBS 20:18 (NIV):
Make plans by seeking advice; if you wage war, obtain guidance.

PROVERBS 17:14 (NIV):
Starting a quarrel is like breaching a dam; so drop the matter before a dispute breaks out.

MATTHEW 8:15-16 (NIV):
Watch out for false prophets. They come to you in sheep's clothing, but inwardly they are ferocious wolves. By their fruit you will recognize them. Do people pick grapes from thornbushes, or figs from thistles?

PROVERBS 20:19 (NIV):
A gossip betrays a confidence; so avoid a man who talks too much.

Chapter 17: WILL GETTING HELP SAVE MY RELATIONSHIP?

MATTHEW 6:33-34 (NIV):
But seek first his kingdom and his righteousness, and all these things will be given to you as well. Therefore do not worry about tomorrow, for tomorrow will worry about itself. Each day has enough trouble of its own.

MATTHEW 7:24-27 (NIV):

Therefore everyone who hears these words of mine and puts them into practice is like a wise man who built his house on the rock. The rain came down, the streams rose, and the winds blew and beat against that house; yet it did not fall, because it had its foundation on the rock. But everyone who hears these words of mine and does not put them into practice is like a foolish man who built his house on sand.

The rain came down, the streams rose, and the winds blew and beat against that house, and it fell with a great crash.

Chapter 18: MOVING FORWARD

JAMES 1:2-8 (NIV):

Consider it pure joy, my brothers, whenever you face trials to many kinds, because you know that the testing of your faith develops perseverance. Perseverance must finish its work so that you may be mature and complete, not lacking anything. If any of you lacks wisdom, he should ask God, who gives generously to all without finding fault, and it will be given to him. But when he asks, he must believe and not doubt, because he who doubts is like a wave of the sea, blown and tossed by the wind. That man should not think he will receive anything from the Lord; he is a double-minded man, unstable in all he does.

JAMES 1:12-18 (NIV):

Blessed is the man who preserves under trial, because when he stood the test, he will receive the crown of life that God has promised to those who love him.

When tempted, no one should say, "God is tempting me." For

God cannot be tempted by evil, nor does he tempt anyone; but each one is tempted when, by his own evil desire, he is dragged away and enticed. Then, after desire has conceived, it gives birth to sin; and sin, when it is full-grown, gives birth to death.

Don't be deceived, my dear brothers. Every good and perfect gift is from above, coming down from the Father of the heavenly lights, who does not change life shifting shadows. He chose to give us birth through the word of truth, that we might be a kind of firstfruits of all he created.

ABOUT THE AUTHOR

Harold L. Turley II was born and raised in Washington, D.C.
An author and performance poet, he lives with his children
in Maryland. Turley first thrilled readers with the critically
acclaimed novels *Love's Game*, *Confessions of a Lonely Soul*
and *Born Dying*. He is also a contributing author to
A Chocolate Seduction and the upcoming *It's a Man's World*.
Visit the author at www.myspace.com/haroldturley2.